Kalevala Guide

To Mount – Hermonite
friend Max,

Tmis

Helsinki, July 11, 2017

Irma-Riitta Järvinen

Kalevala Guide

Finnish Literature Society • Suomalaisen Kirjallisuuden Seura

Helsinki • 2017

2nd revised edition

This book was produced by the Kalevala Society.

Suomalaisen Kirjallisuuden Seuran Toimituksia 1276, Tieto

English-language editing by Leila Virtanen
Layout & illustration by Henriikka Salonen

www.finlit.fi / books
ISBN 978-952-222-193-3
ISSN 0355-1768
Print: Jelgava Printing House, Riga 2017

Contents

» The Great Pike (1945), by Erkki Tanttu (1907–1985).

Introduction

The *Kalevala* (1835, 1849), by Elias Lönnrot, is probably the best known and certainly the most widely translated work of Finnish literature. The work's enduring popularity raises an interesting question: how is it possible that this book, honoured by the solemn epithet 'the national epic of the Finns', continues to fuel the creative imagination? What is it about the Kalevala that keeps on attracting and inspiring new generations of readers and artists?

The world of the Kalevala is mythical – not historical. Therefore, its stories cannot be connected to actual places or events. Essentially, it lives in the realm of the mind's eye. Lauri Honko, a Finnish scholar of the Kalevala, writes: 'Many of the stories and their details become easier to understand if we do not try to force them onto the level of historical time and everyday experiences but try to listen to the voice of myth as it speaks to the man who conceives time as mythical.'

For example, let us consider the Sampo. In the Kalevala, the Sampo is not only a concrete and tangible thing that is made, a 'machine', but also a very abstract, inexplicable symbol, a source of wealth and well-being. The Kalevala is based on verbal art and the power of poetry – on what can be made with words. Full of imaginative leaps and magic, its stories have the power to generate countless images.

The 'heroes' of the Kalevala are profoundly human in their behaviour and weaknesses. Kai Nieminen, a poet who has retold the Kalevala in present-day Finnish (1999), explained his experience of the epic: 'Lönnrot's Kalevala is not pompous and holy; it is funny, exuberant, full of joys and sorrows, smiles, teasing, hidden irony, politics and lyrics.'

J. R. R. Tolkien, one of the greatest European storytellers of the twentieth century, was truly enthralled by the Kalevala. As early as 1914, he mentions the Kalevala in a letter to his fiancée, Edith Bratt; years later, he continues to articulate his fascination with the epic in many ways: 'I was immensely attracted by something in the air of the Kalevala…' For example, he was particularly amused by poem 20, in which ale is brewed for a wedding — surprisingly, with the advice of a bullfinch — and then joyfully consumed. The personified beer even demands a song, threatening, 'I will kick my hoops away, my bottom I will force out!' The story of 'the hapless Kullervo' intrigued Tolkien to such an extent that he adapted it into the tale of Túrin Turambar (in *The Children of Húrin*). Tolkien had studied the Finnish language (as well as Welsh and fourth-century Gothic), finding that 'It was like discovering a complete wine-cellar filled with bottles of an amazing wine of a kind and flavour never tasted before.'

> *J. R. R. Tolkien,*
> *one of the greatest European*
> *storytellers of the twentieth*
> *century, was truly enthralled*
> *by the Kalevala.*

For Tolkien, the Kalevala provided a 'glimpse of an entirely different mythological world'. The English poet Keith Bosley, who has translated the Kalevala into English (1989), speaks about the same experience: '– – the main problem translating the Kalevala into English: there is no cultural equivalent. Oral tradition, in which the Kalevala is rooted, is central to Finnish culture but peripheral to English.'

There are two works in world literature for which the Kalevala has served as a model. One is the Estonian national epic, The *Kalevipoeg* (1857–1861), by F. R. Kreutzwald. Kreutzwald was Lönnrot's contemporary and a medical doctor like Lönnrot. Lönnrot met with him briefly in Estonia in 1844. The epic's main character is the giant hero *Kalevi-poeg*. The story is based on Estonian folk songs and narratives that were worked into a poetic form. Compared to the Kalevala, it is at a greater remove from folk poetry because the author not only invented characters with no folkloric counterparts but also composed lines of his own. When the *Kalevipoeg* was published, Estonian culture was dominated by the country's German-speaking elite. Thus the *Kalevipoeg* became an immensely important book in Estonia, giving rise to a sense of national feeling and identity, as well as inspiring Estonians to start collecting folk poetry and folklore.

The American author Henry Wadsworth Longfellow published his poem *The Song of Hiawatha* in 1855 – only six years after the new version of the Kalevala had appeared. Longfellow's work imitates the trochaic metre and style of the Kalevala. Keith Bosley has stated: '*Hiawatha* just won't do. It trots; the *Kalevala* dances.' The story of Longfellow's epic is based on North American Indian myths and legends. Its narratives mainly tell the legends about Manabozho, the hero of the Ojibwa Indians, not about Hiawatha, the Iroquois chief, as Longfellow had mistakenly thought. At the end of the epic, from his deathbed, the hero and leader Hiawatha wants his people to follow the noble and righteous teaching of the white invaders.

Some decades ago, many Finns were uncomfortable with their national epic. Their qualms about the Kalevala, however, were due to the way the national epic had been taught in school. Pupils had been expected to learn long Kalevala poems by heart and recite them in the classroom. The aims of educators backfired. Indeed, many people found that they could not even bring themselves to touch the book after their school years. The situation is different today: the Kalevala is now far more accessible to readers of all ages. There are humorous websites about the epic for young children; there are Kalevala-inspired comic books – even Donald

》 Elias Lönnrot in his prime, at the age of 43, portrayed in a drawing by G. Budkowski (1845). Four years later, Lönnrot married Maria Piponius and became a father of five children. Only one of his children, a daughter named Ida, outlived him. Finnish Literature Society.

Duck has been caught up in the Sampo adventure. A popular children's book by Mauri Kunnas, *The Canine Kalevala*, came out in 1992. Kirsti Mäkinen retold the *Kalevala* in prose form for children; her book, *The Kalevala – Tales of Magic and Adventure*, appeared in English translation in 2009.

For a long time, a misconception prevailed among the public in Finland about the Kalevala and its relation to folk poetry. This is called 'the romantic conception' – the idea that the Kalevala was a shattered epic, whose scattered fragments were later simply collected from the mouths of the people and put into a book. While it is true that the Kalevala is firmly based on folk poetry, the work is the result of the conscious efforts of its writer, Elias Lönnrot. He devised the plot, built the story and created a set of compelling characters. The amazing thing is that Lönnrot, who collected the poems from the singers, learnt the language of folk poetry so well that he thought of himself as one of them: 'I became a singer myself.'

With the Kalevala Elias Lönnrot sought to paint a picture of Finland, in which the era of heroes, shamans and magic is coming to an end and the new Christian era is beginning. He was determined to create a history for the Finns, a people whose literate culture was still in an early phase of development, and whose

With the Kalevala Elias Lönnrot sought to paint a picture of Finland, in which the era of heroes, shamans and magic is coming to an end and the new Christian era is beginning.

knowledge about the past was vague. Thus, the Kalevala gradually came to have an immense impact on the development of a Finnish national identity, which means that it later had political significance, contributing to the establishment of an independent nation (1917). Now Finnish culture could clearly stand apart from that of Sweden and of Russia.

Nowadays, the issue of national identity is no longer in the foreground – because it already has been fully acknowledged. Today, the Kalevala is more compelling as a literary work that can inspire and challenge artists, writers, musicians and scholars in Finland and beyond.

Artistic interest in the Kalevala has waxed and waned over the decades. After the Second World War, there was a fairly long period of relative indifference to the epic, but interest gradually revived during the 1970s. Artists working in various mediums are currently drawing their inspiration from the Kalevala. It keeps on emerging in new modes of expression: in modern dance and theatre, in rock music, jazz, in comics and children's books.

The language of the Kalevala is varied and rich. It is based on the eastern (Karelian) dialects of Finnish. Although the sentence structures are clear, the vocabulary poses a challenge to present-day readers, for the world of the Kalevala seems so removed from our own. Fortunately, 'Kalevala dictionaries' help to understand the archaic or simply alien language of the epic.

Elias Lönnrot signed the preface to the Kalevala on February 28, 1835. This day has been commemorated as Kalevala Day and the Day of Finnish Culture for one hundred years.

The Kalevala has come to be woven into the fabric of modern Finnish cultural life and even business since the end of the nineteenth century. There are the insurance companies Ilmarinen, Tapiola, Pohjola and Sampo (also a bank), not to mention a newspaper called Kaleva and an asphalting company named Lemminkäinen. The name Sampo is also associated with an icebreaker, a harvester and serves as a trademark for matches. Kalevala Koru produces high quality jewellery and Väinämöinen's Coat Buttons are tasty rye crisps. Names from the Kalevala are commonly used as first names (e.g. Väinö, Sampo, Seppo and Ilmari for males, Aino, Marjatta, Annikki and Kyllikki for females) and place names (e.g. Tapiola, Metsola).

Elias Lönnrot signed the preface to the Kalevala on February 28, 1835. This day has been commemorated as Kalevala Day and the Day of Finnish Culture for one hundred years. After the first edition of the Kalevala, a new, more expansive version was published in 1849; this is the book that is usually referred to when we speak about the Kalevala.

Thousands of pages have been written about the Kalevala, mainly in Finnish. The challenge here is to deal with that vast body of writing, focusing on the main points without losing the charm of details. I have drawn from previous research for this book, but I have chosen to mention the names of writers only in direct citations or in specific contexts. The purpose of this booklet is to provide basic information about the Kalevala in a condensed and easily accessible form. Of course, I hope that this summary would whet the reader's appetite for more of the knowledge and pleasure offered by the epic.

》 Matchboxes with kalevalaic names and figures for advertising various enterprises and organisations were sold at grocery stores and restaurants.

Plot and contents of the Kalevala poems

Plot outline

The plot of the Kalevala is fairly complicated. However, it is made of passages or sequences of poems that revolve around one main character or focus on a course of events. Keith Bosley suggests that the contents of the epic can be divided into cycles according to the main actor in the following way:

> The first Väinämöinen cycle: poems 1–10,
> the second Väinämöinen cycle: 16–25,
> the third Väinämöinen cycle: 39–49.

> The first Lemminkäinen cycle: 11–15,
> the second Lemminkäinen cycle: 26–30.

> The Kullervo cycle: 31–36.

> The Ilmarinen cycle: 37–38.

> The Marjatta cycle: 50.

*The following outline provides
a little more detail:*

Poems 1–2: Väinämöinen's birth, the origin of the world, and the beginning of growth.

Poems 3–5: Joukahainen and Väinämöinen's singing match. Aino's fate and death.

Poems 6–7: Joukahainen tries to kill Väinämöinen. Väinämöinen's visit to Pohjola.

Poems 8–9: Väinämöinen's knee is wounded and healed.

Poem 10: The Sampo is forged by Ilmarinen.

Poems 11–15: Lemminkäinen: courting in Pohjola, killed, resurrected.

Poems 16–17: Väinämöinen looking for spells: in Tuonela, inside Vipunen.

Poems 18–19: Väinämöinen and Ilmarinen wooing one of the daughters of Pohjola.

Poems 20–25: The wedding at Pohjola: preparations, wedding celebrations at the houses of the bride and the bridegroom.

Poems 26–30: Lemminkäinen: kills the master of Pohjola, escapes to Saari, from where he must flee.

Poems 31–36: Kullervo: as a serf in Ilmarinen's house, takes revenge, seduces his sister, kills himself.

Poem 37: Ilmarinen makes the golden maiden.

Poem 38: Ilmarinen courting at Pohjola. Turns the maiden of Pohjola into a seagull.

Poem 39: Väinämöinen, Ilmarinen and Lemminkäinen set out to steal the Sampo.

Poems 40–41: The first kantele is made of pike bones and played by Väinämöinen.

Poems 42–43: The Sampo is stolen. The struggle with the mistress of Pohjola (Louhi). The Sampo is destroyed.

Poem 44: The birch-wood kantele is made and played by Väinämöinen.

Poems 45–47: Louhi's revenge: sends diseases, sends a bear and hides the sun and the moon.

Poems 48–49: Fire is caught by Väinämöinen and Ilmarinen. The sun and the moon are released.

Poem 50: Marjatta and her son. Väinämöinen leaves.

Contents

1   The singer recounts how he learnt his songs. He describes the origins of the world and of the universe. Ilmatar (the Air Virgin), descends to the waters, becomes pregnant from the wind and turns into the Water Mother. A goldeneye lays its eggs on her knee. The eggs break and the world, the sun, the moon and the stars are formed from their pieces. She shapes the earth. After her long pregnancy, Väinämöinen is born.

2   Väinämöinen calls Sampsa Pellervoinen to sow the trees of the forest. An oak tree grows so tall that it blots out the sun and the moon. A tiny man rises from the sea and fells the giant oak, allowing the sun and the moon to shine again. Väinämöinen cuts down a forest, makes the first burnt-over clearing and sows barley. A birch tree is left to grow for the birds, for the eagle to perch on and for the cuckoo to call from.

3   Väinämöinen becomes famous for his songs and wisdom. Young Joukahainen from the North becomes envious of him, challenges him in a singing and wisdom contest and is defeated. The angry Väinämöinen uses his magic to make him sink into a swamp. Fearing for his life, Joukahainen promises his sister's hand in marriage to Väinämöinen. When Aino hears about the promise, she bursts into tears, but her mother is happy about the prospect of a famous son-in-law.

4   While mourning her fate in the forest, Aino meets Väinämöinen and refuses his proposal. She runs home in panic. Aino's mother tries to encourage her to dress up and adorn herself. Aino roams the forest in despair, reaches the seashore, glides into the water and drowns. A hare takes the message to Aino's mother, who begins to cry. From her tears, rivers start to flow, islets are formed, birches grow on them and cuckoos start to call, echoing her sorrow.

5   Väinämöinen goes to the sea to look for Aino. He catches a fish and is about to kill it, but it turns out to be the drowned girl transformed into a fish. Mocking him for failing to recognise her, Aino returns to the sea. Väinämöinen feels sorry for himself, but his dead mother – from the water – advises him to woo a girl from Pohjola (Northland).

6   Väinämöinen rides towards Pohjola with his magical horse. Joukahainen, eager to avenge his sister's death, decides to kill Väinämöinen in spite of his mother's warnings. He shoots Väinämöinen's horse at sea with his arrow. Väinämöinen falls into the sea and is carried by the waves. Joukahainen's mother condemns her son's deed.

7   The grateful eagle rescues Väinämöinen from a watery death and takes him to the shore of Pohjola, where Väinämöinen is left to long for home and cry. Louhi, the mistress of Pohjola, hears him sobbing. She promises to take care of him and feed him, to give him one of her daughters and to send him home, as long as he promises to make her a Sampo. Instead, Väinämöinen pledges to send the smith Ilmarinen to Pohjola, for he has the skills to forge the Sampo. Louhi promises her daughter to the one who forges the Sampo. Väinämöinen is allowed to return home.

8   On his way home, Väinämöinen meets the beautiful maiden of Poh-
     jola and proposes to her. She agrees to marry him, but first wants
     Väinämöinen to perform a few impossible tasks, such as making a
     wooden boat out of the bits of her spindle. Väinämöinen gets to
     work, but his axe slips and blood runs from his wound like a stream.
     Finally he finds an old man who promises to stop the blood flow.

9   Väinämöinen tells the old man the incantations about the origin of
     iron. With these spells the wound is healed.

10   Väinämöinen returns home. He tells smith Ilmarinen to go to Poh-
     jola, to forge the Sampo and to marry the maiden of Pohjola as a
     reward. Ilmarinen is unwilling to go. Väinämöinen deceives him and
     sends Ilmarinen to Pohjola with magic means. Louhi, the mistress of
     Pohjola, treats him well, and Ilmarinen agrees to forge the Sampo.
     The Sampo is made, and it includes three mills that grind flour, salt
     and money. Louhi is pleased. She hides the Sampo inside a rocky
     hill, behind nine locks. Ilmarinen woos the maiden of Pohjola, but
     she rejects him. Ilmarinen returns home feeling dejected.

11   Lemminkäinen sets off to woo Kyllikki, the famous maiden of Saari
     (Island), who has many suitors. His mother warns him not to go,
     for she fears the girls there might laugh at him. Lemminkäinen tra-
     vels to Saari, where he is hired as a herder. He amuses himself with
     the girls, but fails to impress Kyllikki. He abducts her and takes her
     away on his sleigh. They promise to stay together, as long as Lem-
     minkäinen does not to go to war and Kyllikki stays at home. Lem-
     minkäinen's mother receives her daughter-in-law with joy.

12 Lemminkäinen goes fishing but fails to return home in the evening; Kyllikki goes to the village. Their bond broken, Lemminkäinen wants to go to attack Pohjola, against his mother's words of advice. Irritated by her severe warnings, he departs, leaving his brush as an omen: if the brush begins to bleed, he is dead. Lemminkäinen strengthens himself with incantations, enters Pohjola and bewitches the people of Pohjola to faraway places. Only one person, a cowherd, does not fall under his spell; he begins to build up hatred towards Lemminkäinen.

13 Lemminkäinen asks Louhi for her daughter; she refuses, reminding him that he has a wife at home. Lemminkäinen keeps insisting, so Louhi gives him a difficult task: to catch the elk of Hiisi (forest demon).

14 With his incantations to the forest spirits, Lemminkäinen finally catches and kills the elk. Louhi asks him to perform a new task: to bring her the brown gelding of Hiisi, which he does. The last task is to shoot the swan that swims in the Tuonela River (the border between the land of the living and the dead). Lemminkäinen goes to the Tuonela River, unaware that he has been followed by the vengeful cowherd. The cowherd kills him and throws his body into the river, where it is cut into pieces.

15 Lemminkäinen's mother notices that the brush has begun to bleed. She goes out in search of her son. Louhi admits that she sent him to catch the swan in the Tuonela River. Lemminkäinen's mother asks the trees, the road and the moon to tell her where her son might be. The sun tells Lemminkäinen's mother that her boy is lying dead

in the Tuonela River. She goes to the river and rakes up the pieces of her son's body. She puts the pieces together, bringing him back to life with her incantations and prayers. They go home together.

16 Väinämöinen wants to build a boat. Sampsa Pellervoinen finds him an oak tree from which to make one. Väinämöinen cannot finish the boat, however, because he lacks the magic words. He goes to look for the words in Tuonela (the land of the dead). Although the people of Tuonela refuse to let him leave, he escapes by transforming himself into a snake and swimming through the fishnet in the Tuonela River.

17 Väinämöinen continues his search for the missing spells. He is advised to enter the stomach of the gigantic sage, Antero Vipunen, who has long been dead and is covered by trees. Väinämöinen builds a smithy in the belly of the giant and begins to hammer away. Vipunen wakes up. After a while, Vipunen sings all the secret incantations to him and lets him go. Väinämöinen steps out from the giant's mouth and finishes his boat.

18 Väinämöinen sets sail to Pohjola to woo Louhi's daughter. Ilmarinen's sister, who happens to catch sight of him, goes to tell her brother about Väinämöinen's voyage. Smith Ilmarinen, who has made the Sampo and to whom the girl has been promised, goes after him. They both arrive in Pohjola, where Väinämöinen proposes to the maiden.

19 The daughter of Pohjola chooses Ilmarinen, who then has to perform difficult tasks set by Louhi. With advice from his bride, he is able to successfully fulfil the tasks: to plough a field teeming with vipers, to hunt down the bear of Tuonela and the wolf of Manala

(another name for the land of the dead), and to fish the great pike out of the Tuonela River. Louhi gives her daughter to smith Ilmarinen. Beset with sorrow, Väinämöinen returns home. He cautions old men against competing with young men for the favour of young women.

20 Preparations for the wedding at Pohjola begin. The slaughter of an enormous ox by a tiny man from the sea means plenty of meat. Beer and foods are prepared. Invitations are sent to all – except for Lemminkäinen.

21 The bridegroom and his wedding party arrive in Pohjola. Food and drink is served to the guests in abundance. Väinämöinen entertains the guests with his singing.

22 The bride is prepared to leave the house of her father and mother. The days of her childhood are praised, and her future in the bridegroom's house is described. The bride weeps as she envisages her future life in a strange household, but she is reminded of the goodness of her husband-to-be and the comforts of the new house.

23 The bride is given practical advice about life in the bridegroom's house. A wedding guest, an old woman, tells her own life story and weeps about her fate.

24 The bridegroom is advised on how he should treat his wife in marriage. An old beggar tells his own story of how he succeeded in pleasing his wife. The bride, in tears, bids farewell to her family and to her childhood home. Ilmarinen and his young wife leave Pohjola and ride home to Ilmarinen's house.

» The Girl of Tuoni, by Vertti Teräsvuori, from the exhibition Pre Kalevala, 1997.

25 The bride is greeted in Ilmarinen's house with mockery and praise. An abundant feast begins in Ilmarinen's house. Väinämöinen extols the virtues of the groom in song. He thanks the master and mistress of the house for serving food; he also commends the spokesman, the matron and all the other wedding guests. Väinämöinen leaves the house, but breaks his sleigh on the journey. He needs to return to Tuonela once again for tools to repair the sleigh. Once the sleigh is fixed, he resumes the journey home.

26 Lemminkäinen is vexed about not having been invited to the wedding; nonetheless, he wants to go to Pohjola. His mother warns him

of the perils to be met on such a journey. Lemminkäinen sets off and encounters numerous obstacles on the way: a fiery eagle, a pit of burning stones, a bear and a wolf, an iron fence fortified with snakes and a giant snake. He overcomes all these obstacles with his magic skills and arrives in Pohjola.

27 Lemminkäinen enters the house of Pohjola but is made to feel un-welcome. He demands food and drink, but is instead served a beer tankard full of vipers. Lemminkäinen engages the master of Pohjola in a magical singing contest and a swordfight. Lemminkäinen slays the master of Pohjola, cutting his neck with his sword.

28 Lemminkäinen flees from the Pohjola house and returns home to his mother, who soon finds out what has happened. She advises him to flee over the seas to Saari (Island), where his father too once sought refuge.

29 Lemminkäinen travels to Saari; once there, he meets the maidens of the island. After declaring himself a good singer, he is welcomed into their midst. Lemminkäinen enjoys himself with the maidens, having his way with all of them, except for one old maid who then curses him. When the men of Saari decide to kill Lemminkäinen, he must flee again. Lemminkäinen manages to sail off in his boat; he is shipwrecked but then rescued. He finds his way to his mother, who is reduced to hiding in a forest hut after the people of Pohjola had come and burnt their house down.

30 Lemminkäinen wants to take revenge on the people of Pohjola. He takes his friend Tiera with him. Louhi, the mistress of Pohjola, casts a cold spell on them, freezing their boat. Lemminkäinen and Tiera are forced to return home.

31 Two brothers, Kalervo and Untamo, are hostile to each other. Untamo sends his troops to destroy Kalervo's house and people. Only one pregnant woman is spared and taken to Untamo's house. She soon gives birth to a boy, who is called Kullervo. The child, who incidentally happens to be endowed with superhuman powers, is set on taking his revenge. Untamo tries to kill him but fails, keeping the boy as his serf. Kullervo is given various tasks, but he violently botches up each and every one. Eager to rid himself of the boy, Untamo sells Kullervo as a serf to smith Ilmarinen.

32 Ilmarinen's wife makes Kullervo work as a cowherd. She bakes a loaf of bread for Kullervo to take with him to eat while out in the forest. She bakes a stone inside. Uttering protective incantations, she sends her cattle to the forest.

33 While cutting the bread given to him by Ilmarinen's wife, Kullervo breaks his knife on the stone within. Enraged by this insult and the destruction of his knife, Kullervo drives the cows into the swamp and brings home a pack of bears and wolves. Ilmarinen's wife mistakes them for cows, and tries to milk them. She begs Kullervo to undo his charms but is mauled to death by the beasts.

34 Rejoicing, Kullervo flees Ilmarinen's house, while the smith mourns the death of his wife. Kullervo laments his own life, longing to take revenge on Untamo. From the thicket, an old woman clad in a blue coat tells him that his parents are still alive, hiding in the borderlands of Lapland. Her directions lead him to his parents. His mother tells Kullervo that his sister went berry-picking in the forest and never returned.

35 Kullervo's father puts him to work, but the boy messes everything up. His father then sends him to pay the taxes. On his way back, Kullervo meets a girl and seduces her. The next morning they find out that they are brother and sister, for she is the girl who has been lost in the forest. She runs into the river and drowns herself. Kullervo weeps bitterly. He goes home to tell his mother what has happened. She advises him to go and hide himself for a while; still, Kullervo remains bent on taking revenge on Untamo.

36 Kullervo asks his family members whether any of them will mourn him if he dies. Only his mother responds, saying that she would cry. Kullervo, on his way to settle his score with Untamo, receives news that his entire family has died. After crying over the death of his mother, Kullervo then goes and kills Untamo's folks and burns down their houses. He returns home to find the place empty and desolate. Kullervo takes his dog and heads into the forest, back to the spot where he had seduced his sister. He kills himself with his sword. Väinämöinen hears about Kullervo's death and makes this pronouncement: a mistreated child can never grow up to be a man of understanding.

37 Smith Ilmarinen mourns the death of his wife. Lonely and grieving, he decides to forge himself a new mate, a woman made of gold. After a few unsuccessful efforts he manages to make his golden bride. When he gets into bed with the golden bride he finds her chilly and unresponsive. Ilmarinen offers his bride to Väinämöinen, who rejects the offer; Väinämöinen then cautions his people against worshipping gold or wooing women of gold.

38 Ilmarinen travels to Pohjola to woo the younger sister of his dead wife. Both Louhi and the maiden reject his proposal. Ilmarinen ab-

ducts the girl, stealing away with her in his sleigh. The girl is full of despair. They stay overnight in a village, and while Ilmarinen sleeps, the girl amuses herself with other men. When Ilmarinen wakes up and discovers what has happened, he uses his spells to turn her into a seagull. Ilmarinen comes home and tells Väinämöinen that the people of Pohjola are wealthy and living well because of the Sampo. He also tells Väinämöinen what he did to the girl.

39 Väinämöinen gets the idea of stealing the Sampo from Pohjola. Ilmarinen forges a magic sword, and Väinämöinen finds a boat bemoaning its fate, for it has not been at sea for a long time. Väinämöinen pushes the boat to the sea; his song fills it with people. They set off at full speed, with Ilmarinen rowing and Väinämöinen steering. Lemminkäinen happens to catch sight of the boat from ashore; he is called to join them.

40 Using his incantations, Lemminkäinen helps steer the boat through fiery rapids. The boat gets stuck on a rock, which turns out to be an enormous pike. Väinämöinen kills the pike with his sword. The fish is cooked and eaten; then Väinämöinen builds the kantele instrument out of the pike's jawbone. The strings are made from the hairs of Hiisi's (demon's) gelding. Though they try, others are unable to play the kantele. The instrument is brought to Väinämöinen.

41 Väinämöinen plays the kantele. His playing arouses great joy among all living things; animals, birds and spirits of nature gather round to listen to him. All the listeners begin to cry, including Väinämöinen himself. His tears flow into the sea; the goldeneye fetches them, for they have turned into pearls.

42 Väinämöinen, Ilmarinen and Lemminkäinen row to Pohjola to steal the Sampo. Louhi arms her troops. Väinämöinen lulls the people of Pohjola to sleep with his kantele playing. The Sampo is firmly rooted in the rocky hill of Pohjola, but Lemminkäinen ploughs its roots with an ox, enabling them to carry the Sampo to the boat. On the way back at sea, Lemminkäinen begins to sing, but he wakes up a crane at Pohjola; the bird cries out so loudly that the people of Pohjola are awakened. Louhi sends obstacles to block their way and raises a storm, but the raiding seafarers survive.

43 Louhi and her troops pursue the invaders. Väinämöinen uses magic to raise a rock in the sea, causing the people of Pohjola to shipwreck. Louhi transforms herself into a giant bird of prey and collects her troops under her wings. A fierce battle ensues. Drawing his paddle from the sea, Väinämöinen crushes Louhi and her men. The Sampo falls into the water and breaks into pieces, increasing the wealth of the sea. Though Louhi is beaten, she threatens to avenge Väinämöinen and his people with troubles. Carrying only the lid of the Sampo with her, she returns to the now impoverished Pohjola. Väinämöinen finds some fragments of the shattered Sampo; he sows them, giving growth to barley and rye. Väinämöinen prays for good fortune, prosperity and happiness for Finland.

44 Along with the Sampo, the fish-bone kantele has been swallowed by the sea. Väinämöinen searches in vain for his beloved instrument. Pausing to listen to the sorrows of a birch, he then fashions a new kantele from birch wood. He makes the strings from the hair of a young maiden. When he plays, men and women, animals, and all of nature rejoice.

45 Louhi sends 'nameless diseases' to wreak devastation on the people of Kalevala. Väinämöinen first fortifies himself in the sauna with incantations, and then heals the people.

46 Louhi sends a bear to kill the Kalevala cattle, but Väinämöinen slays the bear. A bear-killing feast is organised with songs in praise of the bear.

47 As Väinämöinen plays the kantele and sings, the sun and the moon come to listen to him. Louhi catches the heavenly bodies and hides them inside a mountain. She also steals fire from the people of Kalevala, leaving them in complete and utter darkness. Ukko, the supreme god, makes a spark of fire. The spark falls down from the heavens. After reaching the earth and scorching vast tracts of land, it finally sinks into the Alue Lake. A whitefish swallows the spark, a salmon swallows the whitefish, and a pike swallows the salmon. Väinämöinen and Ilmarinen make a net and try to catch the pike.

48 A better net is made of linen. With the help of a tiny man from the sea, Väinämöinen gets a good catch and finds the pike. He cuts the fish open and discovers the spark of fire, which burns not only his beard but also Ilmarinen's cheeks and hands. Väinämöinen catches the fire and places it in the service of the people. Väinämöinen heals Ilmarinen's burns.

49 The world is still dark. Ilmarinen forges a new sun and moon, but they do not shine. Väinämöinen travels to Pohjola to find out where the sun and the moon might be. He hears the truth from the men of Pohjola, fights with them and finds the mountain where-

in the heavenly bodies are imprisoned. He cannot open the lock. Ilmarinen forges him a set of keys. Louhi, in the form of a hawk, comes to Ilmarinen's smithy. Ilmarinen tells her that he is forging a chain to restrain the mistress of Pohjola. Frightened, she releases the sun and the moon from their prison. Väinämöinen and Ilmarinen are pleased; they greet the sun and the moon.

50 Marjatta, a chaste and virtuous maiden, lives in the house of her mother and father. She goes to the forest to herd the cattle. Marjatta sees a lingonberry, eats it and becomes pregnant. Her parents accuse her of being a whore. They do not prepare her a sauna for giving birth, nor does the wife of Ruotus (Herod). Marjatta finds a stall on the Tapio Hill. The good horse breathes steam on her as she gives birth to a son on the hay. Marjatta takes care of her baby boy, concealing him from the eyes of others. While she is combing her hair one day, the baby disappears. She goes to look for him, asking the star, the moon and the sun if they know of his whereabouts. She finally finds him in a swamp. When Väinämöinen condemns the fatherless child to death, the baby miraculously speaks out, blaming Väinämöinen for the fate of Aino. The boy is baptised by Virokannas and made King of Karelia. Väinämöinen, angry and ashamed, departs in a copper boat, predicting that one day he will again be needed to make a new Sampo. He disappears, leaving the kantele and the songs for his people.

The singer concludes his singing with apologies, just in case he sang too long or too poorly. Yet he asserts himself as the one who blazed the trail for later singers, and hopes that the generations to come will have even better songs and singers.

》 The village of Venehjärvi, in Archangel Karelia, the land of lakes, rivers and forests. The tall forest on the right is the site of the village cemetery. Photo: I. K. Inha, 1894. Finnish Literature Society.

Protagonists and places

Aino

Aino is Joukahainen's younger sister, whom Joukahainen promises in marriage to Väinämöinen in order to save his own life (poem 3). Lönnrot created her story from various folk poems. There is no mention of a female figure called Aino in the collected folk poetry. Aino is Joukahainen's 'only sister'; Lönnrot made her name from the word *ainoa*, meaning 'the only one'. After refusing to marry old Väinämöinen, Aino accidentally drowns herself (4); in the original folk poem, the girl hangs herself. Väinämöinen tries to find her, but he is too late: she has transformed into a fish that mocks him (5). Lönnrot drew from his knowledge of lyric folk poetry to portray Aino's desperation and her mother's sorrow upon the girl's death.

Annikki

The sister of smith Ilmarinen, Annikki, is washing clothes when she spies Väinämöinen's boat at sea; she realises that he is going courting at Pohjola. Aware of the rivalry between her brother and Väinämöinen, she immediately informs Ilmarinen (poem 18). The name Anni (or Annikki) appears in many folk poems, also as the name of Joukahainen's sister, which became Aino in the Kalevala. The name Annikki comes from the name Anna, the name of Saint Anne, Mary's mother, known from apocryphal writings and the tradition of the Christian church.

She became an immensely popular saint in the Western Church from the fourteenth century onwards, and she was also recognised in the Eastern Church. Anni (also Annikki or Annikka) appears in Karelian hunting charms; hunters prayed for her assistance in catching game. Because Lönnrot's aim was to present a 'pagan' world, he erased her name with its Christian connotations from that context in the Kalevala.

Hiisi

Hiisi means either a place or an evil creature. In the Kalevala, Hiisi lives in the forest and is the owner of an animal (e.g. an elk, a gelding, a foal or a hound). Since Christian times, Hiisi has come to be equated with the devil. Originally, the word *hiisi* referred to a sacred grove of pre-Christian times, a holy place set apart from the secular world.

Ilmarinen

Smith Ilmarinen, Seppo Ilmarinen, 'the everlasting craftsman', appears in more than a half of the poems of the Kalevala. He may be considered a culture hero; a skilful craftsman, he learns to use iron, he forges the Sampo, he makes the golden bride and frees the heavenly bodies from the mountain. He takes part in the expedition to steal the Sampo. Ilmarinen is married to Louhi's daughter for a time, and, in his anger, transforms another daughter of Louhi into a seagull. In the folk poems, he is also known as the smith who forged the heavens. Although Ilmarinen has a talent for making things, he is not renowned as a great singer or orator. He is Väinämöinen's helper. The Finnish word for the air, *ilma*, is the stem word for his name, which is one of the oldest Finno-Ugric names for a god.

Ilmatar

Ilmatar, the Air Virgin, descends from the sky to the waters, where she gives birth to Väinämöinen and the goldeneye lays its eggs on her knee (poem 1). In the folk poems, it is Väinämöinen who raises his knee from the water for the seabird to lay its eggs on. The name Ilmatar is known from healing charms. In Karelian epic poems, a maiden called Iro is the mother of three heroes: Väinämöinen, Joukamoinen and smith Ilmollinen.

Joukahainen

Joukahainen is a young man from the North who envies Väinämöinen's status as a singer and sage. The brash young man challenges the older man to a battle of wisdom and knowledge, but loses, pleading for his life (poem 3). His sister, Aino, whom he has promised to Väinämöinen, refuses to marry the old man; she ends up drowning (4). After suffering such defeat, humiliation and loss, Joukahainen resolves to kill Väinämöinen but fails (5). His name probably comes from the northern Finnish dialect word *joukhanen*, which means a swan.

Kalevala

Kalevala is the region led by Väinämöinen (the place names Väinölä, Päivölä, Suomela and Luotola have been used for it in the folk poems). The name Kalevala (meaning a place) is extremely rare in Finnish folk poems. However, Kaleva is a well-known name in Finnish mythology; giants have been called 'Kaleva's sons', and the word appears in the names of constellations. There may be an old Baltic connection to the name Kaleva; Latvian folk poems feature a hammering smith (the Lithuanian word *kalvis* and the Latvian word *kalejs* both mean 'smith'). In his epic, Lönnrot constructed Pohjola (Northland), the site of the people of Pohja, to represent a counterforce, and later an adversary, to Kalevala (the site of the people of Kaleva).

Kullervo

The section about Kullervo (poems 31–36) forms a long epic sequence (2196 lines) in the Kalevala. Lönnrot constructed it from several independent epic folk songs. Kullervo, a miraculously strong child, is the son of Kalervo, who is slain by his brother Untamo. The boy is brought up in Untamo's house as a servant. Untamo attempts to kill him but fails. Kullervo is sold to smith Ilmarinen to work as a serf. Ilmarinen's wife bakes a stone inside his bread. Outraged by this insult, Kullervo drives the bears and the wolves to kill her. Kullervo finds his family alive (this is an illogical twist in the plot). He unknowingly seduces his own sister, takes revenge on Untamo's household and then kills himself with his sword. By skilfully combining several folk poems (e.g. the poem of Kaleva's Son and the poem of Tuurikkainen, the latter is based on a Scandinavian ballad), Lönnrot was able to create a psychologically convincing character, the most well-known tragic hero in Finnish literature. The fate of Kullervo made an impression on J. R. R. Tolkien, inspiring him in his creation of Túrin Turambar in *The Children of Húrin*. Kullervo's name is a derivate of the word *kulta* meaning gold or dear.

Kyllikki

Kyllikki lives on Saari (Island). Though famed for her beauty, Kyllikki is a difficult conquest, thus presenting Lemminkäinen with a challenge. He abducts her and takes her to his home on his sleigh (poem 11). Their bond (the promise to remain at home) is soon broken; Lemminkäinen leaves Kyllikki with his mother, setting off to do battle with the people of Pohjola (12). The epic folk poem depicts her, more clearly than does Lönnrot's text, as a strong-willed and fearless woman opposed to her husband's warlike ways.

Lemminkäinen

Like Kullervo, 'wanton Lemminkäinen' is the main character in a whole sequence of poems (11–15). He is also known as Kaukomieli and Ahti Saarelainen. After abducting and forsaking Kyllikki, he then proceeds to Pohjola to woo the daughter of Louhi. He succeeds in catching the elk of Hiisi and harness its gelding. He is killed and thrown into the Tuonela River, but is rescued and brought back to life by his mother. Lemminkäinen kills the master of Pohjola, escapes to Saari, has his way with the maidens of the island and is forced to flee. He goes to take revenge on the people of Pohjola, later joining the expedition to rob the Sampo from Pohjola. In sum, Lemminkäinen is a fearless risk-taker, an avid fighter and ardent lover. In fact, he botches up the scheme to steal the Sampo by singing so badly that the people of Pohjola wake up. The word for love, *lempi*, is embedded in Lemminkäinen's name. His mother is, after all, the woman of his life. The folk poems at the basis of the Lemminkäinen sequence include both shamanistic elements

» Lemminkäinen´s mother, by Akseli Gallen-Kallela (1897). Lemminkäinen was rescued from Tuonela, the Land of the Dead, by his mother, who put the pieces of his body together and brought him back to life with her prayers and incantations (poem 15). The artist painted his own mother's features onto the face of Lemminkäinen´s mother. Finnish National Gallery, Central Art Archives.

and motifs from medieval visionary literature (e.g. crossing the fiery pit and rapids, overcoming the fiery eagle, the snake fence and beasts, as well as drinking the tankard of vipers). The poem depicting Lemminkäinen's death and resurrection shares similar elements from the Osiris-myth, the Scandinavian Balder-myth and the myth of Christ. Nonetheless, it is worth noting that Lemminkäinen's mother does not bring her son back to life in the epic poems performed by some eminent Karelian singers.

Louhi

Louhi, the mistress of Pohjola, is Väinämöinen's most formidable opponent. Because Lönnrot fashioned this character from such conflicting elements, she emerges as a contradictory figure in the Kalevala. Louhi plays an active role in the following episodes: having the Sampo forged (poems 7 and 10), giving tasks to suitors (poems 13–14 and 19), organising the wedding at Pohjola (20–24), chasing the robbers of the Sampo (42–43), sending diseases and bears to Kalevala, stealing fire from the people of Kalevala, as well as hiding and releasing the sun and the moon (45–47, 49). Lönnrot took the name Louhi from charms or from one oral epic poem, and used it as a name for the mistress of Pohjola. In folk poetry, she is referred to only as 'the mistress of Pohjola' or 'the whore, mistress of Pohjola' (in charms) or 'the gap-toothed hag of Pohjo'.

Louhi appears as a gracious and hospitable hostess at the wedding of Pohjola. Yet for Lönnrot to show the antagonism between Kalevala and Pohjola, he needed to underscore the malevolence of this female character; indeed, he found this evil connection in the charms depicting 'the whore, the mistress of Pohjola', as the source of diseases. At the beginning of the Kalevala, Louhi bears no ill will to Väinämöinen or his people. After the loss of two daughters to Ilmarinen and the slaying of her husband by Lemminkäinen, however, she grows to hate the people of Kalevala. What is more, she also suffers the loss of the Sampo, making her desire to take revenge on the people of Kalevala even more understandable. Louhi's equivalents have been found in the *Edda* (Loki) and in the flying dragon of Icelandic sagas.

Marjatta and Marjatta's son

In the last poem (50) of the Kalevala, a new character is introduced: Marjatta, a chaste maiden who becomes pregnant from a lingonberry. Marjatta is harshly censured for her miraculous pregnancy. She looks for a sauna to give birth in, but is turned down by Herod's wife. She finds a stall for giving birth, and a boy is born. Her baby disappears while she is combing her hair. She looks for him and finds the child. Thereafter the figure of Marjatta recedes, with her child quickly assuming the role of main protagonist. The child is baptised by Virokannas and named King of Karelia, leaving Väinämöinen no choice but to retreat. Parts of the Karelian epic folk song cycle describing the Virgin Mary, the birth of Jesus as well as his death and resurrection form the basis for the first part of the Kalevala poem. In composing the latter part of the poem, Lönnrot drew from other sources: for example, the passage in which the small child miraculously speaks, condemning those who have not acknowledged him — a motif used in Christian saints' legends — comes from another epic song called Marketta and Hannus. Poem 50 ends with Väinämöinen's leave-taking; in the folk poem a foundling accuses Väinämöinen of incest, insulting him and compelling him to leave. In Lönnrot's text, however, the child reminds him of Aino's death.

Pohjola

Pohjola (often referred to as Sariola) is the region and the farmstead led by Louhi, the mistress of Pohjola. A dark and dangerous land, Pohjola lies beyond the sea in the faraway North (Northland, Lapland, Darkland). Yet the heroes of Kalevala are irresistibly drawn to Pohjola because of Louhi's beautiful daughters and the wealth-bringing Sampo. Although the wedding at Pohjola is described as a welcoming feast (poems 20–24), the place is otherwise presented with an ominous and unpleasant air – a village of unremitting cold. Not only is the place teeming with witches, but severed heads on stakes also contribute to its ghoulish atmosphere. To be sure, Pohjola's female leadership casts even more suspicion on the place, making it decidedly Other. There are similarities in the folk poems describing the land of the dead, Tuonela and Pohjola.

Saari

Saari (Island) is the former home of Kyllikki, Lemminkäinen's wife (poem 11). It is the place where Lemminkäinen, after killing the master of Pohjola, seeks refuge (29). While there, he sings, cavorts and makes love with the girls of Saari, only to be chased away by the jealous male inhabitants of the island. Many have speculated about the possible 'historical' or real places – namely, Saaremaa Island on the Estonian coast, the Åland Islands or Gotland – connected with the island of the epic.

Sampsa Pellervoinen

At the beginning of the Kalevala, Sampsa Pellervoinen is called upon by Väinämöinen to sow the lands (poem 2). He helps Väinämöinen find a suitable tree for making a boat, and he also fells an oak for him (poem 16). He is a spirit of vegetation and plants. In folk poetry, he is usually called Sämpsä Pellervoinen. This poem of the sower was sung in the *vakka*-ritual of the Ingrians to promote growth and fertility. Ingrians were living on the southern coast of the Gulf of Finland and in the environs of St. Petersburg. The rite survived among the Ingrian Russian Orthodox population until the nineteenth century, fusing with the Christian festival on St Peter's Day, June 29th. The first name Sampsa probably derives from Samson (the strong man of the Bible but also a Russian Orthodox saint), and the second name is a derivative of *pelto*, meaning field.

Tuoni, Tuonela

The land of the dead (also referred to as Manala) is separated from this world by the Tuonela River. Lemminkäinen goes to the black river to shoot the swan that swims there (poem 14), but perishes doing so. Ilmarinen needs to catch the bear and the pike of Tuoni (19). Lemminkäinen's mother goes to the Tuonela River, rakes through its rapids and finds the pieces of her son (15). Väinämöinen visits Tuonela (16) in order to get the missing magic words for finishing his boat.

Although Tuonela resembles this world with its houses, animals and people, it is a cold and uninviting place. The Kalevala mentions a maiden, a boy, a wife, an old man and an old woman. When Väinämöinen arrives in Tuonela, he is reprimanded for coming there alive, without cause; therefore, the people of Tuonela do not let him go back to the land of the living. He escapes them by transforming himself into a snake. The poem is pervaded with shamanistic elements – in particular, the idea of a shaman entering the land of the dead, the other world, in the shape of an animal.

Vipunen

Antero Vipunen is a long-dead giant and sage. Väinämöinen needs to get the magic words for finishing his boat from him (poem 17). Vipunen swallows him. When Väinämöinen's hammering in Vipunen's stomach wakes him from his deathly slumber, Vipunen sings his incantations to him. Shamanistic features structure the plot of this deliciously macabre poem about paying a visit to Vipunen. Väinämöinen's actions are reminiscent of a shaman who falls into trance to enter the other world and obtain knowledge from the dead. Lönnrot incorporated the longest section of incantations into this poem.

Virokannas

Virokannas baptises Marjatta's son in poem 50. Although his name is somewhat mysterious, it does have associations with vegetation and growth. This name is related to the promoter of the growth of oats in Mikael Agricola's list of 'old Finnish gods' from 1551. His role as baptiser links him to a Christian saint, most probably Saint John the Evangelist. The Karelians burnt incense in oat fields on his memorial day.

Väinämöinen

Väinämöinen, also known as Väinö, 'steady old Väinämöinen', 'the ever-lasting singer' and 'the eternal sage', is the leading figure of the epic, appearing in most of the poems of the Kalevala: 1–10, 16–21, 25, and 35–50. His name originates from the word *väinä*, which means a broad, slowly running stream or straight. Väinämöinen's character is many-layered – and so is the poetry behind him. He is frequently mentioned as an ancient god of the Finns in old Finnish printed literature, first by Mikael Agricola in 1551. Ever since, numerous Finnish scholars have sought to analyse and explain the figure of Väinämöinen; their interpretations include historical, mythical and shamanistic perspectives. Folk poetry about him includes epic poems and charms, and thus his roles are manifold. As a leading figure of the poems, his name has attracted functions from a variety of layers of culture. Väinämöinen has been emphasised in different ways in the various areas of Finnish-Karelian oral singing culture. Lönnrot has combined all of Väinämöinen's roles in his epic. He is the creator god of the world, the one giving shape to the land and to the sea. In the folk poems a seabird, eagle or goose lays its eggs on Väinämöinen's knee, and Väinämöinen and Ilmarinen together make the spark of fire that escapes but is finally captured. As a culture hero, Väinämöinen makes the first boat and the first kan-tele – as its creator, he is also the most skilled player of the kantele; like Orpheus, he is a singer capable of enchanting humans and animals

Väinämöinen, also known as Väinö, 'steady old Väinämöinen', 'the everlasting singer' and 'the eternal sage', is the leading figure of the epic, appearing in most of the poems of the Kalevala.

alike. As a shaman, Väinämöinen is able to visit Tuonela, the land of the dead, and return home. He also goes to meet the deceased wise man Antero Vipunen. As a powerful singer, he sings Joukahainen into – and out of – a swamp. He longs to find himself a wife. His humanity is reflected in his various attempts to get a female companion: for example, his interest in the young Aino and his courting trips to Pohjola. At times Väinämöinen appears ridiculous: when he is mocked by the fish-Aino for not recognising her (poem 5), and at the end of the Kalevala, when he is accused and made to feel ashamed before a baby (50). In the folk poems, the accusations against Väinämöinen are far more severe: he is accused of incest with his mother, even of sodomy. At the close of the Kalevala, he maintains his status of great singer: he leaves the kantele, music and the noble songs for his people.

《 The Departure of Väinämöinen (1896–1906), by Akseli Gallen-Kallela. The basic view of Lönnrot's epic is depicted here: the world of 'paganism', of magic and heroes represented by Väinämöinen is retreating after the arrival of Christianity. Marjatta (Mary) is holding her baby boy in her arms. The little boy in the centre is utterly captivated by the kantele that Väinämöinen left to his people. Finnish National Gallery, Central Art Archives.

Themes and worldview

Although the fraught relationship between the people of Kalevala and Pohjola is a leading theme in the epic, it is connected to the quest for happiness through material well-being (of which the Sampo is the most important symbol), love and justice. Characters seek to achieve these goals through various means. One of them is magic, the power of the word, which has a central role in the Kalevala. Magic leads to success, unlike violence, which regularly spells disaster. A distinguishing feature of the Kalevala is the animate quality of the natural world and its inhabitants: animals and plants speak and act, and so do objects such as boats and swords.

Bear

The bear is referred to in the Kalevala about sixty times, and no wonder: in earlier times it was a respected and feared animal. Nowadays it is the national animal of Finland. Stone Age weapons found in Finland and Karelia were decorated with the head of a bear or elk. The bear and the elk may have been totemic animals. The bear figures prominently in numerous Finnish-Karelian folklore genres, such as animal tales and charms; of course, the bruin is the main character in poems depicting the bear ritual.

The bear is the central figure in poem 46. Louhi 'raises' the bear by magic means. She sends it to kill the cattle of Kalevala. According to magical thought, it was possible to hurt other people and their belongings by indirect means. In the spring, rites were performed, when the cattle were let out to the forest. Protective charms and prayers were recited and magic procedures were used to keep the cattle unharmed. An example of this ritual can be found in poem 32, when Ilmarinen's wife sends her cattle to the pasture. Lönnrot took the origin myth of the bear, which used to be one of the poems usually performed in the cattle ritual, and incorporated it into the context of Väinämöinen's bear hunting feast.

In the Kalevala, the bear hunt takes place in the winter (as it used to), and the hunter wakes up the sleeping bear with his songs.

The arctic bear ritual has also been richly imbued with drama among the Ob-Ugric peoples. In the Kalevala, the dead bear is carried to the house with cherishing words, and poems explaining the origin of the bear are performed. Lönnrot presents here three variations of the myth of origin: the bear was born from the wool thrown into water; it was born in the dark North; the bear was born in heaven, 'on the shoulders of Otava' (the constellation of the Great Bear). Singers from Archangel Karelia and Finnish North Karelia sang about how the bear was rocked in a golden cradle in heaven, and lowered down to earth with golden chains. Throughout the bear ritual, participants treated the animal with reverence; in fact, singers disassociated themselves from the killing of the bear, suggesting that others had slain the animal or that the creature had somehow caused its own death. The procedure of returning the bear's remains back to nature is meticulously described in the Kalevala. Väinämöinen takes the bones 'on a clean tree, a fir with a hundred sprigs'. This part of the bear hunting rite was performed in order to ensure the bear's rebirth and more bears in the future.

Death

Death is encountered in the Kalevala in a variety of ways – and mostly with violence: as a suicide (Kullervo, and maybe Aino); murder (Lemminkäinen is killed by Pohjola's cowherd, the master of Pohjola is killed by Lemminkäinen and the death of Ilmarinen's wife is instigated by Kullervo); and slaughter (Untamo destroys Kalervo's household, Kullervo destroys Untamo's family). The dead will end up in Tuonela, the place of the dead, which is structurally analogous to the world of the living (there are houses, animals and people), but it is cold and dark.

Families

Although numerous families and relationships between family members are poetically portrayed in the Kalevala, mothers – the mother of Aino, the mother of Kullervo and the mother of Lemminkäinen – emerge as the most powerful figures of the families. The Kalevala poems were filtered from the folk poems through nineteenth-century thinking and values. Lönnrot put his imprint on the family relations of the epic, stressing the mother's importance according to the ideals of the nineteenth-century family. Mothers in the Kalevala try to listen to their children; they console, counsel and caution their children against reckless or destructive behaviour. Hence, their roles have become even more substantial than in the original folk poems. Louhi, the mistress of Pohjola is also a mother. Though her relationship with her daughters receives little attention, she deeply regrets handing her daughter over to Ilmarinen, and refuses to give her other daughter to him.

The relations between fathers and their children in the Kalevala are rather vague and lifeless. While Kullervo's father unequivocally denounces his son, no mention is made of the father of either Joukahainen or Lemminkäinen. The absence of fathers is further underscored by virgin births: the birth of Väinämöinen, and, in the end, the birth of Marjatta's son.

Brother and sister relationships end disastrously for both Joukahainen and Kullervo. Joukahainen treats his sister as if she was his property. The fateful encounter between Kullervo and his sister is more like an accident. Annikki, Ilmarinen's sister, supports and helps her brother.

Feelings

In contrast to the original epic poetry, Lönnrot incorporated more feeling and passionate emotion into the poems of the Kalevala. He did so by drawing heavily from lyric poetry, the language of emotions. As indicated below, the whole scale of emotions is present:

Envy: Joukahainen envies Väinämöinen for his knowledge and fame; Väinämöinen envies Louhi for the Sampo; Louhi envies Väinämöinen (and the people of Kalevala) for their good life.

Rage: Lemminkäinen's rage in Pohjola; Kullervo's rage and revenge.

Anger: Väinämöinen's anger towards Joukahainen.

Shame: Väinämöinen's shame in front of Marjatta's son.

Sorrow: the sorrow of Aino's mother; the sorrow of Väinämöinen; the sorrow of Ilmarinen; the sorrow and despair of Aino.

Jealousy: the men of Saari, because of Lemminkäinen.

Inspiration: Väinämöinen's inspiration as a singer and player.

Love: Lemminkäinen's mother; Kullervo's mother

Erotic desire: Lemminkäinen, Väinämöinen, Ilmarinen, Kullervo, Kullervo's sister, maidens of Saari, the daughter of Pohjola (the one turned into a seagull).

Humour

It is not always easy to identify or even to appreciate all the potential humour to be found in the Kalevala. The reasons are numerous. The epic certainly includes mentions of joy and laughter. What is more, the original folk poetry must have been funny, eliciting laughs when performed by skilled singers. Finding the comic elements was — and remains — the task of the audience. People are amused by different things. The material that is humorous to the present reader may differ from those that entertained Lönnrot and his nineteenth-century readers, not to mention the singers of the folk poems.

One of the humorous elements lies in the hyperbolic treatment of some themes: for example, the exhaustive account of Joukahainen's defeat under Väinämöinen's powerful spells, or the over-the-top description of the great ox's size: 'For a week a stoat turned round in the space of one tether; for a day a swallow flew between the horns of the ox...'

Humour is present whenever characters either make fools of themselves or are ridiculed by others, especially when the target of ridicule is a figure of power, strength or authority. Väinämöinen, the great man of wisdom, is made a fool of by Aino, a mere girl. Indeed, by the end of the epic, Marjatta's baby boy makes the wise old sage feel truly small. Present-day readers may chuckle to themselves at the notion of the widowed Ilmarinen making a golden bride for himself. Upon discovering the coldness of his creation, he hands her over to his friend Väinämöinen. Even the lonely old man discards her, calling the golden thing a 'bugbear'.

Situational humour also features in the Kalevala. Take, for example, the poem about stealing the Sampo from Pohjola. In the end, it is Lemminkäinen's poor singing – after Väinämöinen has forbidden him to make a sound – that catches the attention of a crane. The sound of the bird's 'weird croak' wakes up the people of Pohjola, who then set off to pursue the robbers. This detail, however, was introduced by Lönnrot in order to flesh out the character of the defiant Lemminkäinen. The folk poems are even more humorous: there an ant, 'a pismire, wretched fellow', pisses on the legs of the crane, which then lets out a nasty noise, waking the people of Pohjola. Seemingly inconsequential incidents can set the plot in motion, leading to momentous consequences.

Illness

Folk conceptions of illness are articulated most clearly in two Kalevala poems: Väinämöinen visiting Vipunen (poem 17) and Louhi's revenge by sending illnesses to Kalevala (poem 45). Replete with a variety of charms, these extensive sections reveal ideas about the origin of diseases. There were basically two explanations for disease: Illness was either sent by God, or it was caused by some magic force in the outside world. Human beings were basically powerless to combat diseases sent by God. Diseases originating in the world, however, could be beaten, as long as the original source and its nature could be determined. The evil magic forces could be other people, nature (earth, air, water, forest) and its spirits, or the dead; even holy places, such as village churches (in Orthodox Karelia), could be infectious. According to the folk explanations of illness, some afflictions were possibly caused by offending the spirits. It was the task of the sage or the healer to find out the cause of the disease. When doing this, he had to fortify his own power by boasting. When the origin of the disease had been determined, the disease was verbally banished with powerful images to the place it had come from, for example: 'I will banish you − to the furtherst North, to Lapland's vastness, to the barren glades, to the unsown lands, where there is no moon, no sun nor daylight for evermore' (poem 17).

A long narrative charm, 'The Emergence of Nine Diseases' forms a segment of poem 45. Lönnrot has taken the blind girl of Tuonela ('the worst of Tuoni's daughters, wickedest of death-daughters') from other contexts, turning her into the one who gives birth to nine nasty diseases (stitch, colic, gout, rickets, boil, scab, cancer, plague and one unnamed). In folk poetry the 'hag of Pohja' is the source of diseases.

Väinämöinen, a shaman and a healer, uses charms to fight the diseases Louhi sent to his people. The Ache-girl, who collects the aches and pains and grinds them away with her stone, is a compelling image; indeed, the Ache-girl has an equivalent in Scandinavian mythology. To heal his people, Väinämöinen appeals to God for help, just as healers did with their incantations.

Kantele

The kantele is an instrument with a varying number of strings (5, 8, 10, 12 etc.), which has been known and used by peoples around the Baltic Sea. Earlier kantele instruments were carved into a piece of wood, but some 300 years ago a change occurred: someone built a kantele with planks of wood. The prototype had been known among the Baltic-Finnic ethnic groups for about 2,000 years, and the name kantele has parallels in Baltic languages (Lithuanian 'kankles', Latvian 'kokle'). In the Kalevala, the mythical origin of the kantele is told in the language of poetry. There are two versions of the origin of the kantele: the first one was made out of the jaw of a giant pike, the second one of birch. The fish-bone kantele has its equivalent in the myth of the Celtic lyre, the *cwryth*, which was made out of the bones and sinews of a huge fish. Folk poetry mentions a variety of imaginative materials: all kinds of horns and bones (elk, deer, ram, cow, eagle, duck, finger bones) and parts of fish (fins, salmon tails), birch, oak and maple, even steel. The birch-wood kantele first appears in **Mythologia Fennica** by Christfrid Ganander (1789).

Väinämöinen, as a great singer and kantele player, has been connected with the myth of Orpheus. Although the kantele could be used to accompany singers, it was not customary; however, there is little information on this. The kantele was primarily played by soloist, who improvised an endless continuum of melodies. Players never stopped a string but let it sound until he touched it the next time. The five-string version of the kantele relates to the pentatonic nature of ancient Finnish rune-singing.

The kantele became the Finnish national instrument in the nineteenth century. Elias Lönnrot gave his collection of lyrical folk poems

》 The subtle atmosphere of the kantele music: Iivana Shemeikka is playing for his listeners in Suistamo, Ladoga Karelia. A holy icon can be seen in the corner of the room. Photo: I. K. Inha, 1894. *Suomi Kuvissa*. Helsinki 1896.

the name *Kanteletar*. (The ending *-tar* is the feminine ending in a name.) Nowadays new electric kantele instruments even have 39 strings. Many modern Finnish composers (e.g. Kalevi Aho, Pekka Jalkanen, Pehr Henrik Nordgren) have written music for the kantele.

Myths of Origin

The Kalevala contains many origin myths about various natural and cultural phenomena, namely, the world, fire, iron, beer, the kantele, diseases and the snake. All of these myths constitute the fundamental layer of an ancient Finnish worldview. For example, wise men had to have a command of this knowledge in order to cure diseases. Besides having a mastery of the magical power of the word (i.e. spells, charms, incantations), it was also necessary for the healer to know the ultimate cause of the disease; only then was it possible to eradicate it. Keith Bosley writes: 'The antiquity of Finnish myth is perhaps most evident in spells, in which a shaman would recite to an offending object its history in order to control it.'

In the list above, some of the myths – for example, the origin of the kantele and the origin of beer – are called culture myths. The myth of the origin of iron was used for healing wounds caused by a tool made of iron. The origin of fire was used for healing burns. Knowing the origin of the snake was needed to heal snake bites (the adder is the only poisonous snake in Finland and Karelia).

There are also other myths in the Kalevala: for instance, the myth of releasing the sun and the moon from the mountain of Pohjola. We do not know if this myth narrative was sung in a ritual context. However, if it was, the context might have been the end of the winter, the dark period of the North. When that time is over, the returning light in spring is a source of joy. According to one Ingrian singer, this poem was sung during the Shrovetide carnival in February when people were enjoying sleigh riding; this was the time when the days were getting longer again. Or perhaps the myth could explain the eclipse of the sun?

Nature

In the storyworld of the Kalevala, nature is animate and can even feel compassion for human fates. This is one of the entrancing features of the epic. Animals and plants speak and interact with humans. They offer their help and advice: an eagle strikes the first spark of fire for Väinämöinen, thus helping him to burn the clearing so that seeds of grain can be sowed. A hare takes word of Aino's death to her mother. Without the help of animals there would be no beer in the world.

However, by means of magic, animals can be used as agents of evil deeds (e.g. Kullervo sends bears and wolves to Ilmarinen's house to kill Ilmarinen's wife). Väinämöinen soothes the sorrows of the weeping birch, honouring the tree by making a kantele out it. Väinämöinen's playing of the kantele makes all living beings rejoice, whereas all of nature, even plants and grasses, mourn the death of Kullervo's sister. Other kinds of inanimate phenomena (e.g. a road, a boat, the sun and the moon) are also endowed with the gift of speech.

Of the many birds mentioned in the Kalevala, the cuckoo receives the most attention. Väinämöinen leaves a birch standing in the clearing for the cuckoo to call from and for all birds to rest on. The cuckoo has a special significance in Finnish bird lore. People once listened with great interest to its call; young girls counted the number of times the bird would call to predict the number of years until marriage; older people used its call to count the years of a person's lifetime. The overwhelming sorrow of Aino's mother upon her daughter's death is given further expression when her 'whole body is blighted' by the call of the spring cuckoo.

Religion

Lönnrot erased Christian features – for example, the names of Catholic saints or references to Orthodox Christianity – from the folk poems when he used them in creating the Kalevala. He wanted to construct the world of the old Finnish religion just before the arrival of Christianity. The song material he used had been collected mainly in the nineteenth century, and thus was full of Christian references, especially the charms. Lönnrot explained these as later additions. Thus he replaced the saints' names with the names of the heroes, or with the names of spirits, sometimes with the word 'god', which could mean a god of the old religion as well. Lönnrot believed that the primordial religion of the Finns had been monotheistic, but that they had later developed a polytheistic religion, while still retaining a belief in one chief god. The god of weather in ancient Finnish ethnic religion was Ukko, and 'god' has been used by Lönnrot as a parallel word for the name Ukko. Lönnrot made him the 'chief god' in the Kalevala by generalising some references to him in the folk poems. Lönnrot actually created a 'Finnish Olympus', a system of lesser gods (Tapio, the forest spirit, Ahti, the water spirit, etc.).

An interesting example of Lönnrot's way of working with the Christian elements can be seen in the poem about the oath of Lemminkäinen and Kyllikki (poem 11). In the folk poem, they make their oath in front of a Russian Orthodox icon: 'An eternal bond was formed, an eternal vow was taken before the copper icon: Ahti would not go to war, Kyllikki would not go out.' In the Kalevala, the icon (a holy image of Christ, Mary or a saint) is replaced by the Almighty God.

Sampo

The Sampo-myth is perhaps the greatest mystery in the Kalevala, and through the ages, it has been explained in a multitude of ways. When considering the Sampo, we first need to look at the facts presented in the Kalevala: the Sampo is forged by a smith, a task involving several days of work. It is called 'good'. It has a decorated lid, handles (like a chest) and roots that go deep. It can be moved from one place to another. It grinds plenty of something: to be eaten, to be sold or to be kept at home; it creates wealth and well-being. When it breaks into pieces, even the pieces are powerful: they make the sea 'rich', salty and full of life; what is more, the pieces can be sown to foster even more growth.

In folk poetry, the Sampo appears in the epic poems about Väinämöinen and Ilmarinen, and it is forged as a continuation after the cosmic deeds of creation, which emphasizes its value. According to Matti Kuusi, singers have either explained or transformed the Sampo into a sturgeon, a mill, a boat, an oak, a kantele, a kiln full of game, a bride, a flying creature with toes, a sleigh, an otter, a pole, a tree stump, a castle… Some explanations may be caused by the phonetic similarity of the words. Thus, it becomes evident that there is no simple and undisputed explanation for or meaning of the Sampo. New explanations keep appearing each year, even nowadays. 'The Grotte Song' of the *Edda* has a similar magic mill, which sinks into the sea and grinds salt there.

Today the Sampo is understood as a symbol that has had various meanings in different contexts through the ages; it is a mythical and many-sided image.

Today the Sampo is understood as a symbol that has had various meanings in different contexts through the ages; it is a mythical and many-sided image. The word 'sampo' is related to the word *sammas*, which means a pole or a statue. An explanation (by Uno Harva) connects it to the mythological central pole of the world which is attached to the North Star and around which the stars rotate; a variation of this interpretation explains the Sampo as the mythological tree of life.

Sauna

Even today, the sauna endures as an important feature in Finnish social life and culture, and some of the traditional significance of the sauna can be observed in the Kalevala poems. In the Kalevala, the sauna is heated and the sauna bath is taken to prepare for great events and adventures as a purification ritual. When Ilmarinen decides to go and compete with Väinämöinen for the hand of the maiden of Pohjola, Annikki carefully gets the sauna ready for her brother (poem 18). The description of this particular preparation of the sauna beautifully emphasizes the harmony and appeal of the sauna experience; the water is fetched from a pleasant spring, even the bath-whisks are soft and honey-sweet, and the soap she makes is sparkling and lathering. Smith Ilmarinen washes himself absolutely clean: 'Washed his eyes until they glistened, his eyebrows until they bloomed, his neck until it was hen's eggs, all his body white.' In the wedding passage (poem 23), the bride is advised on how to prepare the sauna for her father-in-law. It was a woman's responsibility to get the sauna ready, carry the water, make the bath-whisks and ventilate the smoke sauna properly before bathing. The sauna was also the place for childbirth; Marjatta looks for a sauna where she can give birth (poem 50). The sau-

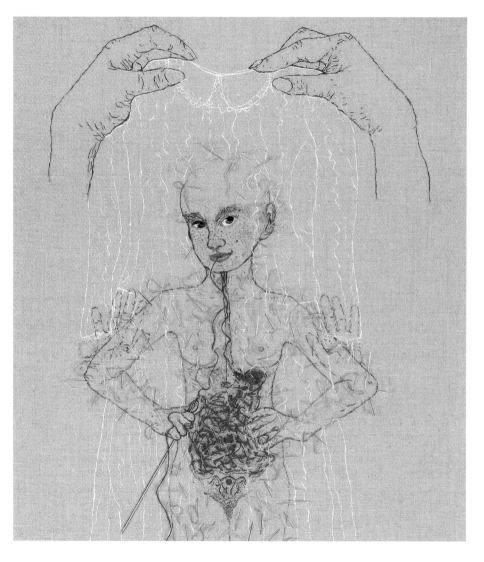

» Marjatta, Viewpoint I, by Ulla Jokisalo (2008; a detail). Finnish National Gallery, Central Art Archives.

na was used for healing rituals, and for love-raising (*lempi*) rituals. It was a place for preparing foods, for example, for making malt and smoking meat.

The sauna as a healing place is exemplified in Väinämöinen's fight against diseases (poem 45). The sweetness of the steam, *löyly* (meaning a soul or spirit in Finno-Ugric languages), is compared to the flow of honey and mead.

Wedding

Lönnrot incorporated a long sequence of wedding poems (21–25) into the Kalevala, illustrating the wedding of Ilmarinen and the daughter of Louhi. He wanted the Kalevala to provide a vivid picture of 'the old Finnish culture'; thus he chose to include a Karelian wedding ritual with many instances of singing, even though its depiction interrupts the epic's flow of events. Lönnrot's poetic construction of the wedding chiefly adheres to the customs practised in Archangel Karelia. Although wedding rituals varied from area to area – for example, on the Karelian Isthmus and in Ingria (the area around St. Petersburg, and on the southern coast of the Gulf of Finland) – there are many similarities among the wedding songs.

The wedding ritual, after the betrothal, followed a certain pattern. It began when the bridegroom and his party, among whom the spokesman was the most important, appeared at to the bride's house to fetch her. The bride's kin welcomed the bridegroom and his people with great kindness and generosity; they also spoke highly of the bridegroom. The bride was made ready, and her future life in the bridegroom's house was described. Laments figured prominently in this part of the wedding. The bride laments her future fate and the loss of her childhood home. There was a saying that if there were no tears at the wedding, there would be many in the marriage. Lyrical poems, songs of sorrow, expressed the wistfulness and sorrow of the bride. Songs of advice for the bride and for the bridegroom were performed. Songs emphasised the importance of treating the bride well – not only by the bridegroom but also by all the members of her new family. Before the departure, the bride sang to her family, thanked them and bade her old home farewell.

The second part of the wedding took place at the bridegroom's house, where many songs were performed. The bride was welcomed with songs, and she greeted her new home. The wedding guests would ask the bridegroom if his visit to the bride's house was successful, and he answered. At the end of the wedding, the participants of the wedding were given thanks: the master and the mistress of the house, the spokesman, the bridesmaids (actually there was an elderly woman and young bridesmaids) and all the wedding guests.

Above all, the purpose of the extensive wedding ritual was to join two families. Essentially, the entire process served to spell out the agreement between the families, which involved giving dowry and an exchange of gifts. Charms and magic were used to safeguard the young couple's happiness. For the bride, the wedding was a rite of passage involving many phases – transforming her from a maiden in her father's house to a wedded woman in that of her husband.

Woman

Although mothers emerge as the most compelling and powerful female figures in the Kalevala, the epic also features active and strong-willed young women — such as Kyllikki (Lemminkäinen's wife), Annikki (Ilmarinen's sister) and the daughters of Pohjola. Even Aino, Joukahainen's sister, who has been romantically idealised by earlier interpreters as a fragile and vulnerable young girl, shows signs of a steely determination and will.

Smith Ilmarinen's creation, the woman of gold, comes across as a truly tragicomic feat. After his wife is slaughtered by wolves and bears, Ilmarinen weeps bitter tears. He then resolves to make himself a new bride of gold. There is poignancy in his endeavour to overcome the irrevocability of death. Yet Ilmarinen's observation — that gold is cold, unlike a human being — and his decision to pass the golden woman over to Väinämöinen produce a comic effect.

The idea of making a female image and longing for 'her' to come to life is expressed in the Pygmalion myth by Ovid in *The Metamorphoses*. Ilmarinen failed, for his golden woman disappointed him with her coldness and inability to respond to him. In the folk poetry, Väinämöinen and Iivana, the Son of Kojonen, also make brides of gold for themselves.

Elias Lönnrot's Kalevala: a work of synthesis

Elias Lönnrot (1802–1884), the author of the Kalevala, was the son of a poor village tailor. He grew up in Sammatti, southwestern Finland. Lönnrot became one of the most widely educated Finnish men of his days, not only in the humanities but also in the natural sciences (e.g. medicine, botany, pharmacy). Yet Lönnrot was also a man of practical intelligence: he worked as a journalist and as a medical doctor. He was an author in the field of popular education, a writer of hymns, a creator of new vocabulary, and the professor of the Finnish language at the university in Helsinki. When speaking of the Kalevala, however, Lönnrot was first and foremost a collector and editor of folk poetry.

With the support of his elder brother and other benefactors, Elias Lönnrot was able to attend school and later pursue his studies at the Academy of Turku, which was the only university in Finland at the time. He studied a variety of subjects: medicine, Latin, Greek, history and literature. During his student years he became acquainted with a circle of students and teachers who were actively interested in promoting the status of the Finnish language. One of them was his teacher, Reinhold von Becker, who allowed Lönnrot access to his own collections of folk poetry and notes on mythology. Lönnrot's doctoral dissertation was called *De Väinämöine priscorum Fennorum numine* (About Väinämöinen, the ancient god of the Finns 1827). Later that same year, the city of Turku burnt down, the university ceased to function for a year and a half and was thus relocated to Helsinki. Lönnrot started his medical studies, writing his doctoral dissertation on the folk medicine of the Finns.

Lönnrot adopted the idea of northeastern Karelia as the land of old songs from a publication by Z. Topelius (the Elder). When Topelius passed away, Lönnrot felt that he could take on the task of compiling a publication of old Finnish folk poetry. This became practically feasible once he began going on collecting trips, for among the people he was able to enter the world of living folk poetry and learn to understand its archaic and sometimes esoteric language.

Altogether, Lönnrot made eleven collecting trips to meet with singers of poetry and write down their repertoires of the ancient oral tradition. Each year, between 1828 and 1844, he travelled more than a thousand kilometres on foot, on skis, by boat or by sleigh. The total distance of his travels has been estimated to be about the same as from Finland to the South Pole. He wrote down more than 3,500 folklore texts representing various genres; he also wrote travel reports, diaries and letters about his eventful journeys. Travelling to the east was relatively easy in Lönnrot's day, for Finland was then a part of the Russian Empire, as an autonomous Grand Duchy, since being ceded from Sweden in 1809.

Lönnrot's first journey into the Karelian hinterland in 1828 was very productive thanks to his meeting with Juhana Kainulainen, of Kesälahti, Finnish North Karelia. Kainulainen sang about Lemminkäinen, the golden maiden, the singing contest, nameless diseases and about stealing the Sampo; Kainulainen's real speciality, however, was the incantation. Another outstanding singer that Lönnrot considered to be Kainulainen's equal was Arhippa Perttunen, whom he met in Latvajärvi, Archangel Karelia, in 1834. At the time, Lönnrot was working as the district medical officer in Kajaani, which was not very far from the villages in Arch-

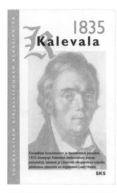

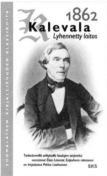

 Covers of various Kalevala
editions and children's books.

angel Karelia, an area with a rich and vital oral tradition. It was here that Lönnrot met and collaborated with the most gifted singers, and this was his usual destination for collecting folklore.

The founding of the Finnish Literature Society in 1831 – Lönnrot was its first secretary – provided him with some financial, but more moral support for collecting folk poetry.

Now, after the fact, it is intriguing to follow how Lönnrot's ideas about an epic started to develop and how they gradually evolved. Making the Kalevala was a long process. As early as 1828, Lönnrot started to edit his collections of poems for printing. He saw publication as a means to preserve the poems not only as evidence of the old ways but also as compositions with real poetic value. Four booklets with the name *Kantele* were published between 1829 and 1831; the fifth never saw publication. His method was to combine manuscript texts on the same subject in order to make more unified and easily readable poems. This ran counter to the guidelines set down by his eminent predecessor, Professor Henrik Gabriel Porthan (1739–1804), who strictly advocated a faithful rendering of poems noted down into print.

The next stage in Lönnrot's endeavours to render oral poetry into literature involved the figure of Lemminkäinen and his exploits. Lönnrot interpreted two characters from the folk poems, Lemminkäinen and Kaukomieli, as one and the same, and he combined the poem texts to make an 825-line story. It was followed by two other collections revolving around a single character and theme, in the same year: *Collection of Poems about Väinämöinen* and *Wedding Songs*. The former was actually taking shape as an epic; it has many of the basic elements of the Kalevala, though with some conflicting features. In 1833, Lönnrot had met the singer Vaassila Kieleväinen, a man who sang and spelt out a chronology for the Väinämöinen-poems that had a tremendous impact on Lönnrot's shaping of the plot. By now, Lönnrot was convinced that he

Elias Lönnrot's Kalevala: a work of synthesis

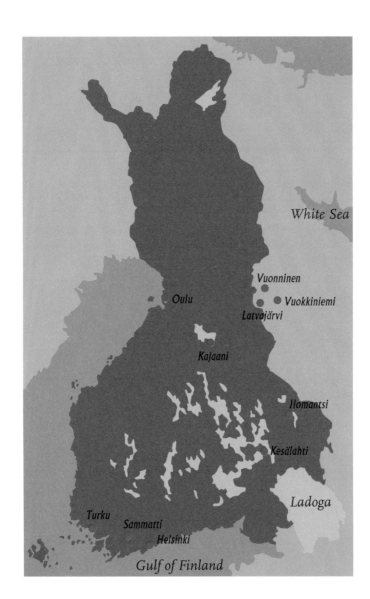

wanted to create a coherent plot with events in chronological order, 'like in the Icelandic Edda', as he states in a letter. Behind this ambition was a hunch about the existence of an actual heroic past — that the songs described the deeds of real people, not faint gods. Other distant models for Lönnrot, besides the *Edda*, were the *Odyssey* and the *Iliad*; the digressions interrupting the momentum of the basic story line in the Kalevala (e.g. the Lemminkäinen cycle and the Kullervo cycle) were presumably adopted from the Greek epic.

Eager to obtain additional material for his story, in 1834, Lönnrot set off to Archangel Karelia on his fifth collecting trip. This expedition proved to be very auspicious: he met Arhippa Perttunen, perhaps the best singer of all, as well as some other skilful singers. Lönnrot wrote down numerous excellent and detailed variants of poems he already

《 In Elias Lönnrot's day, Finland was an autonomous Grand Duchy of Russia from 1809 until 1917.

》 Finland in present-day Europe.

knew in addition to some completely new poems. After returning home, Lönnrot quickly settled down to work. The manuscript was completed in February of 1835, and Lönnrot signed the preface on February 28, which is now celebrated as Kalevala Day and Day of Finnish Culture. This version of the Kalevala is currently known as the 'old Kalevala', because Lönnrot completed another more extensive edition in 1849.

When the Kalevala was first published (in two parts, the first part in December 1835; the second part in March 1836), it included 32 poems and 12,078 lines. Only 500 copies were printed, and selling them took more than a decade. Nevertheless, the Kalevala was enthusiastically received among the fairly small academic circles; what is more, Lönnrot's epic attracted the critical attention and acclaim of leading Finnish and European scholars.

Väinö Kaukonen has estimated that the folk poetry material known and used by Lönnrot amounted to approximately 40,000 lines. Most of it consists of epic poems and charms, about 17,500 lines each; lyrical poems comprised about 5,000 lines. Half of the poems came from Archangel Karelia (in Russia), the other half from Finland (Finnish North Karelia, Ostrobothnia and Savo). Prior to Lönnrot, there were other collections of folk poetry (by Z. Topelius, K. A. Gottlund), but these were not very extensive, and the manuscripts preserved in the collections of the Academy of Turku were lost in the devastating fire of 1827.

Lönnrot published an extensive edited anthology of lyrical folk poems, The Kanteletar, 1840–1841, as well as a collection proverbs and riddles.

Lönnrot wrote an apologetic preface to his book. Despite his fears about the work being criticised for being unfinished, Lönnrot had been anxious to make the poems available to a reading audience. This desire included the idea of continuing to pursue the work; and so he did, in his energetic way. After publication of the Kalevala, Lönnrot kept on collecting more folk poetry. He also had access to collections made by other field researchers. Lönnrot published an extensive edited anthology of lyrical folk poems, *The Kanteletar*, 1840–1841, as well as a collection of proverbs and riddles.

Lönnrot's new edition, the one we know today as the Kalevala, came out in 1849. The epic had grown substantially. There were 50 poems, reaching up to 22,795 lines of verse. The poems about Kullervo had expanded remarkably, now forming a unified tragedy, thanks to the new epic materials collected by Daniel Europaeus in Ingria and Ladoga Karelia. Europaeus had also found his way to Finnish North Karelia, namely, to the village of Mekrijärvi in 1845, where he discovered a thriving singing culture. Europaeus wrote down epic poetry and charms, especially from Simana Sissonen. These materials greatly benefitted Lönnrot's work. Lönnrot added parallel lines, charms and lyrical poems to the earlier Kalevala text. Numerous commentators have described the old Kalevala as an essentially Karelian (Archangel Karelian) epic with closer ties to folk poetry, whereas the new Kalevala has been regarded as a step towards a literary epic.

An oft-asked question concerns the origin of the lines in the Kalevala. Do they count as authentic folk poetry, or are they the product of Lönnrot's creativity? According to Väinö Kaukonen, who has given the question serious thought, there are four kinds of lines in the Kalevala: first, those which are similar in the epic and in folk poetry (33 %); second, those which Lönnrot has changed, in terms of orthography, language, or metre (50 %); third, those lines that can not be found in the folk poems, but are made from the wordings of folk poetry (14 %); fourth, lines made by Lönnrot, or which have no equivalence in folk poetry (3 %). However, the percentages do not tell us everything. Lönnrot approached his work with creativity: he shaped the structure and the characters, fashioning an entire imaginative world.

The Kalevala process, as it has been called, involved many stages. Lönnrot laboured continuously on his Kalevala text. In 1862, he released a shorter version of the epic, meant for schools. This volume only contained about 10,000 lines; to be sure, Lönnrot had re-edited the most violent and erotic scenes (e.g. Kullervo meeting his sister).

The publication of the Kalevala (1835) was noticed abroad. Thanks to Matias Aleksanteri Castrén's early translation into Swedish, Jakob Grimm, the founder of German philology and scholar of mythology, was able to read Lönnrot's epic. In 1845, he spoke appreciatively about the Kalevala to an audience in Berlin; Grimm went into detail about its contents, and understood it as a mythical epic about gods, telling about more ancient times than the times of the heroes. Though Grimm's views differed from Lönnrot's, his speech made the Kalevala known in the literary circles of Central Europe and convinced Lönnrot's Finnish contemporaries of the value of his work.

《 The seal of the Finnish Literature Society (established in 1831) was designed by the artist Magnus von Wright. The text of the seal reads 'Stay holy in Finland'. Today the Society continues to function as a private cultural and research organisation. The Society has an extensive research library, folklore and literature archives, a publishing house, a research department and an information centre on Finnish literature.

》 Lönnrot's field note from Arhippa Perttunen's Sampo-poem in 1834. The line drawn by Lönnrot means that he has used this text when working with the Kalevala. Finnish Literature Society.

...api loukhileuuu legoeta

Oibienta Olka paacta

Koueldi kaeu vay.

Sellen vouy Vy

Zorhu fonum laiuejilla

Kouuuenin veefilla kaau

40 Siella kulhi 6 ruohta

Suila 7- kefea

kulhi kauferla 4

Petnjaula palhyu paaua

Vhia tijuurteloapi

45 Udhva ruhuuloopi

Pauaqueta
Pavau naerk paluelva

Narta uhho huuri huu

Kalevala-metre folk poetry
and its context

To create the Kalevala, Lönnrot drew upon the archaic Finnish and Karelian sung poetry and charm tradition. Initially it was known as Finnish poetry or ancient Finnish poetry, but it later came to be called kalevala-metre poetry. It was cast in trochaic tetrametre, which has been estimated to have developed about 1000–500 B.C. among proto-Finnic groups living near the Gulf of Finland. Besides the Finns, other Baltic Finnic peoples – namely, Karelians, Ingrians, Votes and Estonians – also used this poetic metre. Although the metre has no rhymes, it uses alliteration and many forms of parallelism. The melodies of kalevala-metre poems covered a narrow range, usually consisting of only five notes.The scale corresponds to that of the five-stringed kantele instrument.

Kalevala-metre was used in epic poems, lyrical poems, lullabies, charms, ritual poems (e.g. wedding songs and songs of the bear ritual), calendar songs, work songs, songs used in folk games, not to mention proverbs and riddles. When Lönnrot formulated a plot for the Kalevala, he combined these various genres of poetry for his own purposes.

Kalevala-metre poems were sung in a special language that Finns and Karelians had mastered centuries ago, though some individuals were more adept at it than others. This so-called kalevala language was learnt in childhood, like any mother tongue. Lönnrot, in his preface to the

Kanteletar, called singing and playing, the musical expression of human beings, 'another, more sacred language'. In western Finland, the kalevala-metre gradually started to vanish at the end of the sixteenth century, and it was slowly replaced in song by rhyming four-line stanzas, a form that was spreading from Scandinavia. In the days of Lönnrot and his contemporaries, in the mid-nineteenth century, the old oral singing culture was alive and well in Eastern Finland, Karelia and Ingria.

There are certain rules in the kalevala language. Presented here are just a few of the most important principles. The kalevala-metre is an un-rhymed and non-strophic trochaic tetrametre. When sung, the lines have four or five stresses, and the range of the melodies tends to be narrow, usually consisting of five notes. The idea of the metre is based on the variation of stress on syllables (strong, weak, neutral), and the position of the syllable in relation to the metre (the foot is rising, i.e. stressed, or falling, i.e. unstressed). The so-called broken lines, in which the stress of the word and the metre do not coincide, add variety and liveliness to the metre; broken lines are more numerous in folk poetry than in Lönnrot's Kalevala. The metre is characterized by alliteration, which can be weak (repetition of the same consonant or vowel) or strong (e.g. 'sanat suussani sulavat', 'the words melt in my mouth'). Kalevala-metre poetry favours strong alliteration (repeating the first consonant and a vowel). Even today Finnish speakers tend to employ alliteration in everyday speech. As for stylistic features, the most dominant ones are parallelism and repetition, and the use of stock epithets (vaka vanha Väinämöinen/steady old Väinämöinen, lieto Lemminkäinen/wanton Lemminkäinen).

When shaping his own kalevala language for the epic, Lönnrot made some changes to the language of the folk poems. First of all, he unified the metre, making it more regular and correct than in the original poems. He added alliteration and parallelism (repeating the idea expressed in the main line). Adding parallelism in lines makes the narration longer, slower and somewhat heavier. In the Kalevala, the idea of parallelism is not only apparent on the level of lines but also on the level of structure: certain motifs and themes are constantly repeated, but with variation. The examples are numerous, but here are just a few: there are three virgin births (of Väinämöinen, of nine diseases, and of Marjatta's son); the heavenly bodies are set free twice; the tiny man rises from the sea to solve problems a couple of times; Väinämöinen powerfully sings three times and shakes the surrounding nature; the mothers of Joukahainen, Lemminkäinen and Kullervo warn their sons against committing potentially fateful deeds; tears fall from the eyes of Aino's mother, and of Väinämöinen; animals help people in various ways, for example, by carrying the news of Aino's death and by fetching yeast for the beer; and both Kullervo and Ilmarinen converse with their swords. Here is an example of the parallel description of crying, of tears falling:

Poem 4 (Aino's mother):

The mother wept, a tear rolled:
her plentiful waters rolled
out of her blue eyes
to her luckless cheeks
to her ample breasts.
One tear rolled, another rolled
her plentiful waters rolled
from her ample breasts
upon her fine hems.
One tear rolled, another rolled
her plentiful waters rolled
down from her fine hems
upon her red-topped stockings — —.

Poem 41 (Väinämöinen):

The waters rolled from his eye
others oozed from the other
dropped upon his cheeks
upon his fair face
down from his fair face
upon his wide jaws
down from his wide jaws
upon his stout breast
down from his stout breast
to his sturdy knees
from his sturdy knees
upon his handsome insteps
down from his handsome insteps
to the ground beneath his feet − −.

What sort of cultural milieu did Lönnrot encounter when he went to
set down on paper the old poetry from eastern Finland and Karelia,
where the old singing traditions were best preserved? Archangel Karelia, where Lönnrot found his best singers, was a thickly forested area
with numerous lakes and rivers. Hunting and fishing were important
sources of livelihood, in addition to small-scale agriculture; itinerant
peddling added income but also meant that many men of working age
left their homes for long periods of time. Villages were situated by rivers or lakes, providing excellent waterways for transport. People were
Russian Orthodox by religion, which was combined with beliefs from
the old ethnic religion (e.g. belief in nature spirits). Old Believers lived

in Archangel Karelia and further south in Olonets Karelia. They were descendants and followers of people who had escaped persecution by the Russian Orthodox Church and the Russian state in the seventeenth century. Separation from the church was connected with changes in religious books and religious practices, for example, the way of making the sign of the cross. Old Believers were committed to maintaining the old practices. Some famous singers, for example, Ontrei Malinen, were Old Believers. For Lönnrot, this expression of Christian faith was quite alien; he made comments and observations about their beliefs and practices in his travel diaries.

Kalevala-metre songs played just as vital a part in everyday life as they did in ceremonial occasions. Weddings were the most important festive events to be celebrated with traditional singing, with both kalevala-metre singing and laments, whereas funerals and memorial rites were accompanied only by laments. But people also sang in everyday situations: when working, passing the time in the evening, during fishing trips, etc. Practically everybody knew how to sing at least a little, but of course some singers were exceptionally skilful and even famed for their talents. Others, however, were known as excellent folk healers who mastered the charms. In many cases singing skills ran in the family – namely, in the Perttunen and Malinen families, in Archangel Karelia, and in the Sissonen family, in Finnish North Karelia.

Kalevala-metre songs played just as vital a part in everyday life as they did in ceremonial occasions.

Kalevala-metre songs are divided into three main categories: 1) epic poems, which tell a story (e.g. about the Sampo, forging the golden maiden or going to Tuonela, the land of the dead); 2) lyrical poems, which express feelings; and 3) charms and ritual poems, the former be-

ing used for a variety of magical purposes and also performed by re-
citing. Ritual poems included wedding songs, bear ritual songs and calendar songs. Lönnrot used all of these genres of poems when creating the Kalevala.

How were the songs performed? For a long time, a misconception
prevailed concerning epic song performance: it was thought that epic
singers performed their songs while sitting face-to-face, holding each
others' hands and making a mechanical 'rowing' movement. Although
photographic 'proof' suggests that performers did sing in a rowing position, this evidence has little to do with ethnographic reality. In fact,
the photographer had been so sure that this was the 'right' way of singing that he had asked the singers to pose in that position. Singers were
mainly men, but women also knew and sang these old songs. If there
were two singers, the main singer would sing a line, and the other singer would join him at the end of the line, and then repeat it by varying
the melody somewhat. As the accompanist was ending, the main singer joined him again at the end of his line and then started a new one.
Of course, the singers may have sat side by side, and they may have
touched the other's hand, but they did not 'row'. Sometimes a kantele
or a bowed harp was played to accompany the singing.

In Ingria (area on the southern side of the Gulf of Finland and
around St. Petersburg), where D. Europeaus collected poems, later used
for the Kullervo-cycle in the 1849 Kalevala, the singing tradition was
dominated by women. The performance situation was radically different
from the ways of performing in the northern areas. The Ingrian poems
were not discovered by Finnish researchers until around the middle of
the nineteenth century, so there is a possibility that male singing had
more or less vanished from the area by then. The Ingrian songs were
performed by a main singer and a female chorus that repeated the lines
after the main singer.

❰❰ Miihkali Perttunen was the son of Arhippa Perttunen, a singer Lönnrot met in Latvajärvi, Archangel Karelia in 1834. Like his father, Miihkali was a great singer. After losing his eyesight at the age of fifty, Miihkali was only able to perform light household tasks. Sometimes he had to go begging. Photo: I. K. Inha, 1894. Finnish Literature Society.

❱ Matjoi Plattonen was born in 1842 in Suistamo, Ladoga Karelia. She became widely known as a lamenter, but she also knew charms and kalevala-metre poems. Plattonen was discovered by a group of artists and folklore enthusiasts. She was not afraid to perform her art in front of large audiences in faraway places; in fact, in the 1920s, she made a trip to Budapest, Hungary, to represent Finland in a Finno-Ugric culture conference. Photo: Samuli Paulaharju, 1907. Finnish Literature Society.

❱ Pedri Shemeikka was born in 1825 in Suistamo, Ladoga Karelia. His handsome figure was often compared to that of the 'old Väinämöinen'. He posed as a model for the sculptor Alpo Sailo. The composer Jean Sibelius met him as well and was deeply impressed. Shemeikka was a man of many talents. He was known as a skilful hunter of bear and deer; he also played the kantele and he was well versed in charms and kalevala-metre poetry. Photo: Samuli Paulaharju, 1907. Finnish Literature Society.

 # Singers

The connection between the poems of the Kalevala and reality was established through the singers whom Lönnrot had met and interviewed on his journeys, and whose songs he actually used for his book.

Although Lönnrot listened to scores of singers during his travels, there are 70 individuals that he met who have later been later identified. He characterised and made notes about 48 singers in his travel diaries and letters, and he mentions 13 of his singers by name. Most of the singers he met and interviewed were men, but he also encountered some outstanding female singers, whose voices can mainly be heard in the *Kanteletar*, a collection of lyrical songs.

Lönnrot crafted many fascinating observations of the singers he met. In the preface to the Kalevala (1849), he divides the singers into two types: those who remember and memorize the songs they have heard and learnt in childhood, and those who have learnt the songs later, in adulthood, but who remember the themes and lend variation to the songs in a creative way. When he was shaping the Kalevala, Lönnrot also came to see himself as a singer, a colleague of the singers he had worked with; thus, he would fall into the latter category. But thanks to the will of the singers who cherished the songs of their elders, poems survived from generation to generation.

The following paragraphs will briefly introduce some of the singers Lönnrot met personally and who were especially important in making the Kalevala. Lönnrot became acquainted with these singers in the midst of their everyday toil: fishing and hunting, working in the fields, logging, weaving and knitting, tending children. He occasionally felt the need to pay his singers, enabling them to take time away from their work to sing for him.

Lönnrot met Juhana Kainulainen in 1828, on his first collecting trip in Kesälahti, Finnish North Karelia. Thanks to his detailed travel diary, we know a great deal about their acquaintanceship and collaboration. At the time, Kainulainen was 40 years old, an active man in his prime. He was, above all, a specialist of charms: healing charms; and charms for hunting the bear and the deer, the fox and the hare, birds and squirrels. These remarkable hunting charms appeal to the forest spirits, which are numerous, both Christian saints and spirits from the ethnic religion. In his travelogue, Lönnrot makes it clear that Kainulainen was an 'enlightened' man and a church board member, who nevertheless considered his charms a 'holy inheritance' from his father, a man once famed as an expert hunter. Kainulainen also sang about Lemminkäinen, thus furnishing Lönnrot with the basic scheme for the Lemminkäinen poems in the Kalevala. His repertoire included wedding songs as well as lyrical songs from a male perspective. In addition to Kainulainen's manly style, Lönnrot plainly appreciated his ability to memorize and preserve the charms and poems he had learnt from his father. Lönnrot thoroughly enjoyed living in Kainulainen's house. Lönnrot's gratitude to the whole family for their kindness and concern for his welfare is apparent in his travel report.

In 1833, in the village of Vuonninen, Archangel Karelia, Lönnrot came to know another able singer. His name was Ontrei Malinen; he was just over 50 years old. Even though he performed only seven or eight poems for Lönnrot, all of them represented the later essential themes of the Kalevala, and moreover, they were clear and aesthetically pleasing poems. His 365-line song about the Sampo amounts to a miniature epic with the following plot: Väinämöinen is shot and he falls into the sea. When he is moving in the sea, the cosmos takes shape: the earth and the sky are formed, islets in the sea, the sun and the moon, and the stars. Väinämöinen ends up in Pohjola, and in order to get back home, he promises that Ilmarinen will come and make the Sampo. The Sampo is then stolen from Pohjola, and the mistress of Pohjola and her men pursue the robbers. A battle at sea ensues, but Väinämöinen defeats her and her people. His last words promise abundant crops and the beginning of agriculture. Three myths of origin are present in this poem: the origin of the world, the origin of the Sampo, and the origin of agriculture, thus emphasizing Väinämöinen's role as a culture hero. Väinämöinen clearly emerges as Malinen's chief hero and the main figure; and so he is in Lönnrot's Kalevala.

Malinen was renowned for being a great wise man and sage. According to the testimony of another singer, Malinen's magic was so powerful that he could sing 'the teeth out of a bear's mouth – and then put them back again'.

According to Lönnrot's writings, Malinen was an accomplished kantele player. Lönnrot was also something of a musician, for he played the flute and the kantele, but he could not write down music from the singers. Nonetheless, his own musicality informed his appreciation of the poetry, making him understand that the vitality of the folk poems arose from the inextricable bond between words and melody.

Lönnrot also interviewed Vaassila Kieleväinen, another inhabitant of Vuonninen, when Malinen had to go fishing. Kieleväinen had been renowned as one of the most powerful wise men in Archangel Karelia, but when Lönnrot met him, he was no longer at the height of his powers.

The most significant outcome of their encounter turned out to be an extensive poem about Väinämöinen. Kieleväinen was a poor singer, whose performance did not flow; in fact, he sometimes had to narrate in speech instead of singing. For Lönnrot, however, what really mattered was capturing the order of events in Kieleväinen's performance. There was logic in the way the poems were linked up to each other – for example, Väinämöinen chasing the 'woman of the water', Väinämöinen in the sea creating the islands and islets, making the golden maiden, Ilmarinen forging the Sampo, followed by wooing at Pohjola, and the wedding thereafter, Ilmarinen's homecoming after the wedding and, finally, Kullervo's revenge on Ilmarinen's wife.

Now Lönnrot had a rough idea of how the poems about Väinämöinen, Ilmarinen and Kullervo could be combined.

In April of 1834, Lönnrot met the greatest of singers, Arhippa Perttunen, of Latvajärvi, Archangel Karelia. Within just a matter of days, Perttunen sang to him long poems in their entirety in a coherent order – over 4,000 lines in total. Arhippa Perttunen was close to 70 years old. He also provided his careful listener with a charming childhood memory: he had gone fishing with his father and with another man. Sitting by the campfire in the evening, the young boy listened to the men talking and singing. They sang through the night,

Prior to the Kalevala's publication, Lönnrot paid little attention to women's songs. Their time came later.

and 'not once with the same words'. In Arhippa's view, the songs and the singers deteriorated since his childhood days. According to his values, the poems needed to be long and slow, and they had to be chaste. His long and beautiful epic songs told about Väinämöinen and Ilmarinen, the Sampo, building the pike-bone kantele and Väinämöinen's skilful playing. He sang about finding the missing words from Vipunen's stomach. He sang about Lemminkäinen's death, and about Tuiretuinen and his sister (this poem was made part of Kullervo's story in the Kalevala). The Song of Mary performed by Perttunen was the Karelian folk interpretation of the birth of Christ – and Lönnrot used parts of it for the final poem of the Kalevala.

Perttunen's poems were metrically almost flawless, and he had a solid command of the poetic language of formulas and parallelism. Lönnrot obtained so much poetic material from him that he could now expand his sketch into a poetic work. In less than year after listening to Arhippa Perttunen, Lönnrot's first Kalevala was completed.

Prior to the Kalevala's publication, Lönnrot paid little attention to women's songs. Their time came later. Nonetheless, Lönnrot did meet with a number of competent female singers; for instance, he appreciated the artistry of Arhippa Perttunen's sister, Moarie, and a famous performer of lyrical songs, Mateli Kuivalatar, in Ilomantsi, Finnish Karelia. Moarie's song about a girl who hangs herself and about her mother's sorrow found its place in the Kalevala, in the Aino-poem.

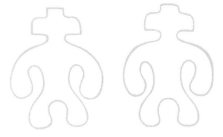

The Kalevala
and other epic models

The Kalevala is a poetic epic. The word 'epic' derives from the ancient Greek word *epos* meaning 'word', 'speech' or 'song accompanied by music'; as a loanword in Latin, it came to mean 'heroic poem'.

What is an epic? The definitions are many. For instance, the anthropologist Brenda Beck has called the epic a 'super story', a long narrative in poetic or prose form. An Indian oral epic studied by Beck also exhibits the following characteristics: it is a narrative performed by professionals; its heroes are considered sacred; it is connected to other mythological and cultural traditions; and its narrators and listeners believe that the events described are true and historical.

The epics of the world have conventionally been classified as either folk epics or art epics; while the former are considered to be derived from folk poetry and myths, the latter are viewed as the artistic creations of individual poets or writers. Yet this dichotomy is misleading: there are also folk epics that may have been composed by a single unnamed poet. Furthermore, even though the poet of the Kalevala is well known, and the book was written to be read, the epic is still based on the norms of oral folk poetry. We know the *Iliad* and the *Odyssey* of the Greeks and the *Beowulf* of the Anglo-Saxons and Germans only in their literary forms, but they also probably evolved through the oral tradition. In the Karelian oral-epic singing tradition, there were clusters of poems forming miniature epics, such as the Sampo-poems, for example.

While it is true that nearly all peoples of the world have been entertained, informed and instructed by epic traditions, only a few of them have had a poet or scribe commit the poems to the written record and shape them into a work of literature.

What do we know about the epic models that Lönnrot had in mind while he was writing the Kalevala? In the preface to the 1835 Kalevala, he clearly articulates the influence of previous collections of folk poetry, for as he read them, he had been inspired to find more poems about Väinämöinen, Ilmarinen and Lemminkäinen, so that 'longer narratives could be written about them, following the models of Greek and Icelandic and other epics'. By the time Lönnrot began his studies at the Academy of Turku in 1822, a lively discussion about folk poetry — especially concerning the originality of *The Poems of Ossian* by James Macpherson (1760–1763) — had already been going on for decades, since the times of Professor Henrik Gabriel Porthan in the 1760s. The theory of the epic, presented by Friedrich August Wolf in 1795, was known and debated about in Turku as well as in other European literary circles. According to this theory, the *Iliad* had its origin in the songs of various oral poets, and at some point one individual skilful singer (Homer) put them together, thus laying down the foundation for an epic, which was later written down and further developed in writing. The earlier, romantic conception of the epic was that the narrative gave birth to itself, as though generated by the collective 'soul' of the people.

A group of enthusiastic young students in early 1800s, who were called the 'Turku Romantics' (A. I. Arwidsson, A. J. Sjögren, A. Poppius and K. A. Gottlund), were keen on collecting folk poetry and publishing the results, if possible. Kaarle Akseli Gottlund was the first person who actually spoke out, in 1817, about the idea of a Finnish epic, 'that would be a new Homer, Ossian, or Nibelungenlied'. The idea was strongly in the air, so to speak, when Lönnrot arrived at the university. Indeed, in 1820, Reinhold von Becker, his teacher of the Finnish language, published an article about Väinämöinen, using all available information in the manuscripts so far about this central character of Finnish epic folk poems. He concluded that Väinämöinen was a historical character. Lönnrot later shared this opinion. While pursuing his studies, Lönnrot became acquainted with research on Homer, and he was also well aware of Wolf's theory of the epic. Lönnrot was familiar with the texts of Homeric epics, and later translated some poetry from the *Odyssey* into Finnish in hexameter. However, there are no discernible loans or passages in the Kalevala that are patterned after the Greek epics. It is another matter that there are certain phenomenological resemblances in the mythologies, for instance, that Orpheus and Väinämöinen are great bards.

Although well-versed in the Homeric epics, Lönnrot did not appear to have any real familiarity with the contents of the German epic *Nibelungenlied* – if so, it was only superficial. In fact, his command of German was quite poor.

As for the Icelandic *Edda*, Lönnrot was fascinated by it. The European literati, especially those in Scandinavia, had discovered the poems of the *Edda* in the early nineteenth century. The poems or songs of the *Edda* are different from kalevala-metre epic poetry in many ways; they are shorter, divided into stanzas, and include direct speech, monologue or dialogue. They are lyrical or dramatic in their expression, and come closer to ballads. In the thirteenth-century texts, the prose of the 'fornaldarsagas' and the poetry of the *Edda* were meant to compliment each other. The story was told in prose, but the poems were intended to provide dramatic and lyrical expression to a moving event – such as

As for the Icelandic Edda, Lönnrot was fascinated by it.

the demise of a hero. However, some structural similarities have been discovered: the beginning of Lönnrot's epic, the birth of Väinämöinen, the creation of the world, and the contest between Joukahainen and Väinämöinen bear a resemblance to the first Odin-poems in the *Edda*; there is, for example, a similar contest in wisdom between Odin and the giant Vafthruðnir. Lönnrot did not pay close attention to the obvious similarities between many themes and motifs in kalevala-metre epic poems and charms and the Scandinavian poetry; these questions have been later taken up and are being currently explored by present-day researchers.

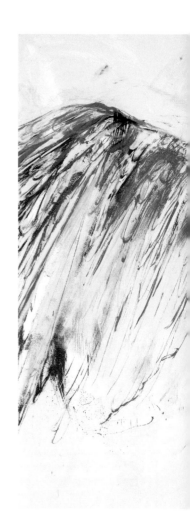

>> Louhi, by Marjatta Tapiola (2008). Finnish National Gallery, Central Art Archives.

The Kalevala and the arts

Like any major literary work, the Kalevala has the ability to stir the imagination — to launch images and create associations. It is no wonder, then, that this book, which is based on folk poetry, has lent inspiration to other modes of artistic expression as well. Nowadays the Kalevala has found its way into a variety of art forms — for example, comics, modern dance, commedia dell'arte and rock music. There seem to be no limits. Since the mid-nineteenth century, the Kalevala has proven to be a tremendously generative force in the world of art. Because so many artists have drawn from its stories, characters and images to make something new, the following presentation can only provide a glimpse of this vast subject matter.

Karelianism

A current of ideas, which was later named Karelianism, prevailed in Finnish art during the last decade of the nineteenth century until the 1910s. The movement was characterised by love for the Kalevala and admiration of the Karelian landscape, which was the home of the kalevala-metre poems. Karelianism was based on the romantic notion that the Kalevala represented the ancient Finnish past, with Karelia as its last sanctuary.

In the visual arts and in architecture, interest and enthusiasm were directed to the decorative motifs of Karelian houses, textiles and household objects. One of the features of this movement was to make holistic works of art; artists such as Akseli Gallen-Kallela and Pekka Halonen built their studios in the Karelian style, and all details in the interiors were made according to their own plans or were handcrafted by the artists themselves. The artists wanted to re-interpret folk models and patterns and import elements of folk art into artistic design. The leading representatives of Karelianism in art were the painters Akseli Gallen-Kallela, Eero Järnefelt and Pekka Halonen, the artist and designer Louis Sparre, the sculptors Emil Wikström and Alpo Sailo, the architects Väinö Blomstedt and Viktor Sucksdorff, the authors Eino Leino and Juhani Aho, and the photographer Into Konrad Inha.

The Kalevala Society was founded in 1911 (officially in 1919) by artists and scholars enchanted by Karelia, its folklore and the Kalevala. The composer Jean Sibelius joined this circle of artists, along with the linguist E. N. Setälä, the folklorist Väinö Salminen, the ethnomusicologist Armas Otto Väisänen, and many others. In 1920, the scholars and artists of the Kalevala Society carried out an ambitious project: a documentary of the Karelian wedding ritual. Filmed in Suojärvi, this was the first long documentary film made in Finland. The music for the premiere showing of the film was composed by Armas Launis.

Literature and drama

The Kalevala became a wellspring of ideas for many Finnish writers. In the late nineteenth century, until the 1910s, the period of national neo-Romanticism or national symbolism prevailed on the Finnish literary scene. Even though Kalevala-inspired writings rarely attained critical acclaim, the phenomenon is significant in terms of the importance and continuity of the Kalevala in Finnish culture. Many writers of that period, who used kalevalaic plots, characters and ideas, adopted the use of the kalevala-metre. Often the use of metre clearly proved to be too difficult, easily becoming awkward and cumbersome in the hands of some authors. For many, it was equally challenging to rewrite kalevalaic subject matter to create new and compelling literary works. There was a tendency to use kalevala themes as allegories of current political events, especially in the time of repression, when the Russian administration in Finland was tightening its hold on Finnish society and culture at the turn of the century. Certain anachronistic features are often present in the use of characters from the Kalevala in later literature.

The figure of Kullervo attracted the most literary attention, especially in the period of national neo-Romanticism in the early twentieth century. However, the first writer drawn to Kullervo was Aleksis Kivi, the novelist, poet, and dramatist, who created exemplary literary works in Finnish at an early stage in the 1860s, when there was essentially no such thing as literature written in the Finnish language.

Kivi had delved deeply into the imaginative universe of the Kalevala. He had attended Lönnrot's lectures about the epic at the university in Helsinki. Kivi's play about Kullervo won a literary prize and was performed on stage in 1860. It was published in 1864. His interpretation of Kullervo was informed by his knowledge of Aristotelian poetics, Greek tragedy and Shakespearean tragedy, especially *Hamlet*. Kivi's Kullervo, a slave but born to be free, is a distinctly modern individual, a young man conscious of breaking the boundaries set for him. He makes his choices with his eyes wide open, except when caught unawares by destiny, as in the tale of Oedipus, and ends up seducing his own sister.

For the poet Eino Leino, the Kalevala was a profound source of inspiration, to which he kept returning. His companions were other prominent artists of the late nineteenth and early twentieth century: Gallen-Kallela, Sibelius, Kajanus, Halonen and Wikström. Leino created a vision of Finnish history through the ages in his long poem, *Tarina suuresta tammesta* ('Tale of the Great Oak', 1896). The great oak here symbolises the long period of Swedish rule, which led the Finns to lose their mythical memory. When the oak is felled, the sun shines again and nature is revived. The Russian tsar Alexander the First appears in an idealised light. He is bringing light and hope for the people, but his oath to the Finnish people is also binding for his followers. His later play, *Sota valosta* ('War for Light') in 1902 is a political drama, defending the national culture against external threat; in those years the Russian repression on Finland was strong.

Leino's most powerful work inspired by the Kalevala is *Helkavirsiä* ('Whitsongs'), which was published in two volumes 1903 and 1916. Although the poet here employs the kalevala-metre and kalevalaic metaphors, its subject matter is different. Leino's heroes are mythical, anguished and controversial. They are defiant of society, convention, enemies and even death. Death is met with bravado and courage, not resignation. However, the latter part of *Helkavirsiä* has a softer tone. The mood becomes melancholic, in-

The figure of Kullervo attracted the most literary attention, especially in the period of national neo-Romanticism in early twentieth century.

cluding myths and cosmic visions. Leino's use of the kalevala-metre is skilful. He has modified the metre by reducing the number of parallel lines; he varies the rhythm and his language is more concise and immediate.

Although novelists and poets virtually ignored the Kalevala during the interwar years, it remained an important frame of reference for patriotic feelings for writers of public speeches and newspaper articles.

The leading modernist poet in the 1950s, Paavo Haavikko, revived the Kalevala as a literary resource. His first Kalevala-inspired book was the extended poem in kalevala-metre, *Kaksikymmentä ja yksi* ('Twenty and one'), 1974, which tells the story of stealing the Sampo. A group of men from the North row to the Byzantine Empire and steal a coin-minting machine from Constantinople in the hope of gaining prosperity and happiness; yet another view among the numerous explanations of the Sampo. Haavikko wrote the manuscript for the television film *Rauta–aika* ('Age of Iron'); it appeared in book form in 1982. The opening of the book is confrontational: 'Forget! Forget the Kalevala, its heroes, words, phraseology; forget what you have heard about them, the pictures you have seen.' Haavikko de-mythifies the heroes of the Kalevala, its shamans and culture heroes: they are human beings, tired, weak and resigned. Directed by Kalle Holmberg, the film 'Age of Iron' raised a heated public – and scholarly – debate on how the Kalevala should be interpreted. In this way, the film and the controversy around it renewed general interest in the epic, opening the way to a variety of views.

Except for the drama *Kullervo* by Aleksis Kivi, which continues to be performed on the stage, not many Kalevala-based plays have endured as successfully to the present day. On the other hand, the past fifty years or so have seen numerous new – and intriguing – renderings of the epic as a whole. The new modern era of Kalevala performances actually started, interestingly enough, not in Finland, but in Hungary, when the Hungarian theatre Thalia and its director Karoly Kazimir staged the Kalevala in Budapest in 1970, and visited the Helsinki City Theatre. The 1980s and 1990s also witnessed a growing number of new interpretations of the Kalevala in Finland: the ballet by Jorma Uotinen in 1985, and various performances of the epic themes on the stage, for example, those directed by Atro Kahiluoto, Samuli Reunanen and Pekka Milonoff. Directed by Davide Giovanzana and Soile Mäkelä, The Kalevala dell'Arte -performance (2008) was spiked with the humour of Italian theatre.

Visual arts

During the last 150 years, the Kalevala has been visualised by nearly 400 artists in roughly 2,500 works of art; in addition to paintings, graphic arts and sculptures, this number also includes illustrations, comics and sketches. Yet Väinämöinen, especially his singing and playing of the kantele, has persisted as the most popular subject over the years.

The first visualisations of kalevalaic themes actually appeared before the publication of Lönnrot's Kalevala. Väinämöinen was understood as an ancient god of the Finns, and as a singer and player comparable to the Greek Orpheus, as a patron of arts akin to Apollo, and as a Promethean provider of fire. Indeed, Väinämöinen was already portrayed by the Swedish artist Eric Cainberg in his relief decorations of the Academy of Turku in 1814. His was the first visual representation of Väinämöinen playing the kantele, symbolising pagan times in the three-part historical relief. In the 1830s, a statue of Väinämöinen by the Danish sculptor Gotthelf Borup was erected in the Monrepos Park in Viipuri.

The first artist to become truly cognizant of the richness and variety of the subject matter of the Kalevala was Robert Wilhelm Ekman. The storyworld of the epic – its characters and events – held Ekman in its thrall. Cosmopolitan by experience and training,

Of all the artists inspired by the Kalevala, Akseli Gallen-Kallela is the one whose work has had the most lasting impact on conceptions and images about the epic.

Ekman had studied in Stockholm and Rome, as well as in Paris, with Paul Delaroche, the celebrated master of historical painting in those

» The master at work: Akseli Gallen-Kallela (1865–1931) painting frescoes with kalevalaic themes onto the ceiling of the Finnish National Museum in Helsinki in 1928.
Here the forging of the Sampo is taking shape. The Gallen-Kallela Museum.

days. Ekman made plans and sketches for a large gallery of kalevalaic paintings, but due to a lack of resources he could never realise it as a whole; at the time, there were some reservations about his style — that it was perhaps not sufficiently 'Finnish'. A leading Finnish critic denounced his art as 'mythological crap'; he also frowned on the nakedness of mermaids in Ekman's paintings. Yet Ekman produced superb paintings of Väinämöinen playing the kantele and of Lemminkäinen's mother in Tuonela, not to mention his rendering of Ilmatar (the Air Virgin); it was only later, however, that his works were given their fair due. A great number of sketches remain of his extensive plans.

One of Ekman's contemporaries, the Swedish sculptor Carl Eneas Sjöstrand, also specialised in Kalevala themes.

Sjöstrand discovered the world of the Kalevala through M. A. Castrén's early translation of the epic into Swedish (1841). He began his kalevalaic sculptures in the 1850s, and moved to Finland in 1863. His artistic construal of topics from the Kalevala was imbued with the ideals of Antiquity. Not even his ethnological expedition to eastern Finland in 1857 can be seen in the details of his sculptures. Although Sjöstrand was primarily interested in representing the masculine epic heroes — namely, Kullervo, Lemminkäinen and Väinämöinen — he also sculpted works depicting Aino and Kyllikki. He enjoyed more success and was granted more respect by his artistic contemporaries than Ekman ever did. Indeed, Sjöstrand's frieze of Väinämöinen playing the kantele found its place in the vestibule of the University of Helsinki in 1866.

Of all the artists inspired by the Kalevala, Akseli Gallen-Kallela is the one whose work has had the most lasting impact on conceptions and images about the epic. The intensity and power of his visions have prompted many later artists to make their own versions, as though to rebel against Gallen-Kallela's art. Gallen-Kallela began to focus his creative energies on the Kalevala in the 1880s, though recognition for his artistic commitment to the epic only came in 1891, the year he won an art competition. Thereafter he began to bring forth his celebrated paintings; a triptych about the story of Aino evolved from an earlier version made in Paris. Gallén's (later Gallen-Kallela) young wife, Mary, was the model for Aino. His greatest works about the Kalevala were created in his studio-home in Ruovesi, far from Helsinki, in the quietude to be found amidst forested landscapes and lakes. These were works called 'The Defence of the Sampo' (1896), 'Lemminkäinen's Mother' (1897), 'Joukahainen's Revenge' (1897), and 'The Curse of Kullervo' (1899). In the 1890s he also produced works of graphic art on Kalevala themes.

The 1900 World Fair held in Paris was particularly important for Finnish artists, because now Finland was presenting itself with a pavilion of its own, with its own identity. The young leading artists of the day planned the pavilion in the National Romantic style. The architect was Eliel Saarinen, who later made a career in the United States with his son, Eero Saarinen. Akseli Gallen-Kallela painted kalevalaic frescoes onto the ceiling of the building. These works have been preserved only in photographs, because the building was torn down when the World Fair was over. Later, as a final and grand work before death, Gallen-Kallela painted themes from the Kalevala onto the ceiling of the Finnish National Museum in Helsinki. These images include: 'Ilmarinen Ploughs the Field of Vipers', 'The Defence of the Sampo', 'The Great Pike' (replacing the theme painted in Paris, 'Christianity Arriving in Finland') and 'The Forging of Sampo'. After the World Fair, Gallen-Kallela continued painting frescoes on kalevalaic themes, for example, 'Kullervo Going to War' (1901), which can be seen in the music hall of the Old Students' House in Helsinki. He produced a number of paintings, wood carvings and etchings dedicated to the Kalevala during the 1910s and 1920s.

Gallen-Kallela had long been dreaming about illustrating and decorating a version of the Kalevala, which would be called 'The Great

» Kullervo, Sinisukka, Äijönlapsi, by Risto Suomi (2008).
Finnish National Gallery, Central Art Archives.

Kalevala'. He finished the illustrations for only four poems. After their completion, he made 'The Decorated Kalevala' (printed in 1922), which was meant to be just a preliminary version for 'The Great Kalevala'. In the end, however, it remained Gallen-Kallela's most complete illustration of the Kalevala. The artist Hannu Väisänen illustrated the Kalevala in 1999.

A number of eminent Finnish artists were interested in the Kalevala, as well as the Finnish landscape and people. The turn of the century, say, from 1880 to 1920, was witness to such an intensive phase of artistic creativity that it came to be referred to as the Golden Age of Finnish art.

Besides Gallen-Kallela, the painters Pekka Halonen, Eero Järnefelt, Väinö Blomstedt and Joseph Alanen all worked with kalevalaic subject matter. The sculptor Alpo Sailo specialised in creating busts of Karelian rune-singers; in fact, the Karelian countryside and way of life were so inspiring for him that he chose to relocate to Archangel Karelia with his family for a few years. The famous female singer from Ingria, Larin Paraske, was portrayed by Albert Edelfelt and Eero Järnefelt. Pekka Halonen made only a few kalevalaic paintings. Joseph Alanen's kalevalaic paintings follow the aesthetic principles of Art Nouveau; highly decorative, they are reminiscent of textile art.

One of the great sculptors of Kalevala-inspired art was Emil Wikström. He won the first prize in the competition for Lönnrot's statue in 1899; the statue was erected in Helsinki on Lönnrot's 100th anniversary in 1902. Wikström used kalevalaic themes in fountains, and made statues of individual characters, such as Kullervo (1889), Väinämöinen (1907), Aino (1916) and Marjatta (1926). Also, Eemil Halonen made a long career as a Kalevala sculptor. After the Second World War, many sculptors have used characters and subject matter from the Kalevala; the most well-known sculptors inspired by the epic would be Sakari Tohka, Viljo Savikurki, Heikki Virolainen and Essi Renwall.

In modern times, the Kalevala and related folkloric materials have continuously provided artists with ideas, images and elemental stories; unlike Gallen-Kallela, however, these artists do not regard the visualisation of the Kalevala as a monumental ambition – it is simply a topic among others. In 2009, the Kalevala Society launched a project called 'The Kalevala of the Artists'. This project assembled twenty artists and composers to produce works from various poetic themes of the Kalevala. The artists were Martti Aiha, Juhana Blomstedt, Ulla Jokisalo, Kuutti Lavonen, Stiina Saaristo, Risto Suomi, Nanna Susi, Marjatta Tapiola, Katja Tukiainen and Santeri Tuori. The composers were Kimmo Hakola, Pekka Jalkanen, Olli Kortekangas, Einojuhani Rautavaara, Herman Rechtberger, Aulis Sallinen, Jukka Tiensuu, Riikka Talvitie, Jovanka Trbojević and Lotta Wennäkoski. The illustrations and the music came out as a book and as a CD (SKS 2009).

Music

It has been recently estimated that the total number of Kalevala-related compositions is about 500. The number has been rising rapidly during the last 25 years. The Kalevala appears to be an intriguing source for composers of the present day. In recent decades, the artistic activity of Finnish composers has increased, especially whenever an anniversary of the epic is being celebrated.

Jean Sibelius wrote his imposing compositions on kalevalaic themes during the same period as Gallen-Kallela was working with his kalevala art. Sibelius was not the first composer to make music based on Lönnrot's epic. In fact, the first Finnish composition with a kalevalaic theme was *The Kullervo Prelude* by Filip von Schantz in 1860 – the same year that Aleksis Kivi wrote his acclaimed play about Kullervo.

The first Finnish composer who wanted to write music focussed on Finnish subjects was Robert Kajanus. He composed his symphonic poem *Aino* (1885) for the celebration of the 50th anniversary of the Kalevala. It ends with the singing of a male choir – in Finnish, which was remarkable at the time.

According to Kalevi Aho, it was hearing Kajanus's *Aino* that compelled Sibelius to turn to the richness of the Kalevala as a source for his music. Sibelius wrote to his fiancée, Aino Järnefelt, in 1891: 'I think that the Kalevala is completely modern. It is all music, I think, a theme and its variations. All actions are governed by the atmosphere, gods are humans, Wäinämöinen is a musician, etc.' Sibelius, whose artistic cohort was made up of Kalevala-inspired friends, wanted to determine what would be especially Finnish in music. He listened to the singing of Larin Paraske, an outstanding female singer from Ingria, and, while on his honeymoon, he also heard singers in Border Karelia. The music of Sibelius does not, however, take direct citations from folk music or oral poems, but he uses their elements to conjure up an atmosphere that has the feeling of being Finnish. Sometimes this feeling is a mythical experience of nature, for example, in *Tapiola* (1926).

Sibelius composed the *Kullervo–symphony* when he was staying in Vienna. First performed in 1892, it was a momentous occasion in Finnish musical life. The parts of the symphony follow the story of Kullervo: 'Prelude', 'Kullervo's Youth', 'Kullervo and His Sister', 'Kullervo Leaves for War' and 'Kullervo's Death'.

Sibelius composed a number of Kalevala-related works: *The Lemminkäinen Series* (four parts) in 1893-1900, symphonic poems *Satu* ('A Fairy Tale'), 1892/1902, and *The Daughter of Pohjola* (1906). *Luonnotar* ('The Nature Spirit') in 1913 is connected to the myth of the origin of the world from the eggs of a seabird. *The Lemminkäinen Series* has four parts, which show great variation in atmosphere, ranging from erotic to meditative: 'Lemminkäinen and the Maidens of Saari', 'The Swan of Tuonela', 'Lemminkäinen in Tuonela', 'Lemminkäinen's Homecoming'. In his old age, Sibelius himself again commended this composition, saying that if Kullervo and Lemminkäinen were counted among his numbered symphonies, he would have nine symphonies altogether, instead of seven.

Sibelius intended to compose an opera based on a kalevalaic theme, but he never managed to carry it out. In 1898, however, Oskar Merikanto composed the first Finnish-language opera called *Pohjan neiti* ('The Maiden of the North'). Armas Launis's *Kullervo* opera (1917) is based on the text by Aleksis Kivi, but Launis wrote the libretto. In his opera, Launis actually used some folk melodies that he had heard on his trips when collecting folk songs.

In 1913, Leevi Madetoja composed his *Kullervo Overture,* which emphasises the tragic fate of Kullervo. He also made several other kalevalaic compositions, such as *Sammon ryöstö* ('The Stealing of Sampo') in 1915 for a male choir, solo singer and orchestra. The leading theme uses a folk melody. The 100th anniversary of the Kalevala was celebrated in Sortavala, Karelia in 1935, and Madetoja composed a cantata called *Väinämöisen soitto* ('The Playing of Väinämöinen') for the festivities.

In the 1930s, only a single composer – namely, Uuno Klami – was able to forge his own musical way and escape the formidable shadow of Sibelius. For Klami, making Kalevala-inspired music was a lifelong work. *The Kalevala series* by Klami (first version performed in 1933) includes four parts: 'The Origin of the Earth', 'Pastorale (Kalevala, The Sprout of Spring)', 'The Lullaby of Lemminkäinen's Mother' and 'The Forging of the Sampo'. In 1943, he composed the fifth part, and reworked the other ones. It took twenty years altogether. *The Kalevala Series* was performed in October 1943, when Finland was at war. Klami has described the starting point of his work: 'I tried to avoid here, as well as in my other compositions, the depressed and deep melancholy which Finn-

》 Covers of CDs by Finnish bands that have been inspired by the Kalevala.
Above left, Värttinä, *Iki* (2003) BMG Finland, cover design Ilkka Kumpunen;
CMX, *Rautakantele* (1995) Herodes, EMI, cover design Tuula Lehtinen;
Amorphis, *Silent Waters* (2007) Nuclear Blast, cover design Travis Smith and
Kingston Wall *III – Tri-Logy* (1994) Zen Garden, original graphics Bruno Maximus.

ish music has been criticised about, especially abroad.' Klami was planning to compose an opera about Väinämöinen, but this plan was never realised.

The opera has been an appealing art form for many later composers inspired by the Kalevala. For example, Aulis Sallinen, using Aleksis Kivi's play, wrote his celebrated opera *Kullervo* (1986–1988). Ilkka Kuusisto's opera *Sota valosta* ('War of the Light') was first performed in 1981. It is based on Eino Leino's text, which combines the themes of stealing the heavenly bodies and releasing them as well as the poem of Marjatta. Einojuhani Rautavaara's opera *Thomas* (1985) touches the kalevalaic theme of the vanishing world of shamanistic beliefs and the arrival of Christianity. Tapio Tuomela's opera *Äidit ja tyttäret* ('Mothers and Daughters'), in 1997–1998, interprets the story of Lemminkäinen. Here the character of Lemminkäinen appears as a spineless failure controlled by the women in his life. The libretto was written by the author Paavo Haavikko. Ballet music on the Kalevala, called *Päivänpäästö* ('The Release of the Sun'), was composed by Tauno Marttinen. The ballet was first performed in 1985.

Pehr Henrik Nordgren's composition *Taivaanvalot* ('The Heavenly Lights') was first performed at the Kaustinen Folk Music Festival in 1985. This work has been inspired by the myth of the release of the sun and the moon, which is narrated in the 49th poem of the Kalevala. Nordgren's music uses a children's choir, singers and an orchestra with folk instruments (e.g. the bowed harp, ram's horn) in a most ingenious way.

The opera *Die Kalewainen in Pochjola* was composed by the German Karl Müller-Berghaus in 1890, but was performed in Turku on the Kalevala Day in 2017 for the first time. The composer had been working in Turku as a musical director when he wrote his opera, influenced by Richard Wagner.

The Kalevala in translation

The Kalevala is the most widely translated book of Finnish literature. It has been translated, in some form or another, into more than sixty languages. The Swedish translation was the first, in 1841.

Translating the Kalevala is particularly difficult because of the metre and the vocabulary, which is not easily comprehensible even to a present-day Finn. There are around 40 full translations of the Kalevala, and very few in the metrical form. Sometimes only a selection of poems has been translated, but it seems that translating a selection of poems has later led to the translation of the whole epic; the Kalevala is a challenge for the translator.

In the list below, a translation of only a selection of poems has been indicated with the word 'parts'. The prose translations of the Kalevala have not been separately indicated. All possible versions that have been published, such as children's versions and other shorter forms and adaptations, have not been listed here, but they are indicated by 'etc'.

In some cases, the translation has been made from another language, not from Finnish. A fairly recent phenomenon is the translation of the Kalevala into various Finnish dialects; this trend shows a genuine and living interest in the epic. These translations, however, are not listed here. The name of the translator is given in brackets.

Лоухи, Похьолы хозяйка,
редкозубая старуха,
тотчас выскочив из дома,
очутилась у калитки.
Напрягает слух колдунья
и слова такие молвит:
«Слышу я не плач ребенка
и не женское стенанье,
этот голос — голос мужа,
бородатого пришельца».

Лодку сталкивает в воду,
ставит легкую на волны,
направляет прямо к Вяйнё,
к мужу, плачущему горько.

Мрачной Похьолы хозяйка
тут над ним запричитала:
«Ой ты, старец злополучный!
Угодил ты на чужбину!»

Мудрый старый Вяйнямёйнен
голову слегка приподнял
и сказал слова такие:
«Я и сам про это знаю —
угодил я на чужбину,
в незнакомую сторонку:
я на родине был знатен,
у себя я был известен».

Лоухи, Похьолы хозяйка,
снова с ним заговорила:
«Ты дозволь мне слово молвить,
дай мне выведать, пришелец,
из какого края будешь,
рода, звания какого?»

Мудрый, старый Вяйнямёйнен
говорит слова такие:
«Обо мне молва ходила,
был по общему согласью
я душой вечерних игрищ
и певцом любого дола

64

» A selection of Kalevala poems in Russian. Edited by O. W. Kuusinen. Translated by N. Laine,
M. Tarasova, A. Titova and A. Hurmevaara. Illustrated by T. Ûfa. Karjala-kustantamo, Petroskoi 1970.

Arabic
1991 (Sahban Ahmad Mroueh)

Armenian
1972 [A. Siras]

Belorussian
1956 parts (M. Mašapa)

Bulgarian
1991 (Nino Nikolov)

Catalan
1997, etc. (Ramon Carriga-Marquès)

Chinese
1962 (Shih Hêng)
2000 (Zhang Hua Wen)

Croatian
2006 (Slavko Peleh)

Czech
1894–1895 (Josef Holeček), etc.

Danish
1907 parts (F. Ohrt)
1994 (Hilkka & Bent Søndergaard)
etc.

Dutch
1940 parts (Jan H. Eekhout)
1985 (Maria Mies le Nobel)

English
1888 (John Martin Crawford)
1907 (W. F. Kirby)
1963 (Francis Peabody Magoun)
1988 (Eino Friberg)
1989 (Keith Bosley), etc.

Esperanto
1964 (Joh. Edv. Leppäkoski)

Estonian
1891, 1898 (M. J. Eisen)
1939, 1959 (August Annist), etc.

Faroese
1993 (Jóhannes av Skarđi)

French
1867 (L. A. Léouzon Le Duc)
1930 (Jean-Louis Perret)
1991 (Gabriel Rebourcet), etc.

Fulani
1983 parts (Alpha A. Diallo)

Georgian
1969 (M. Matšavarjani,
Š. Tšantladze, G. Dzneladze)

German
1852 (Anton Schiefner)
1914 (Martin Buber)
1967 (Lore & Hans Fromm)
2004 (Gisbert Jänicke), etc.

Greek
1992 parts (Maria Martzoukou)

Hebrew
1930 (Saul Tschernichowsky)

Hindi
1990 (Vishnu Khare)

Hungarian
1871 (Ferdinánd Barna)
1909 (Béla Vikar)
1972 (Kálmán Nagy)
1987 (Imre Szente), etc.

Icelandic
1957, 1962 (Karl Ísfeld)

Italian
1909 (Igino Cocchi),
1910 (Paolo Emilio Pavolini),
1986 parts (Gabriella Agrati)
2010 (Marcello Ganassini), etc.

Japanese
1937 (Kakutan Morimoto),
1976 (Tamotsu Koizumi), etc.

Kannada/tulu
1985 parts (Amrta Sōmeśvara)

Karelian (Olonets Karelian, Livvi)
2009 (Zinaida Dubinina)

Karelian (Viena)
2015 (Raisa Remsujeva)

Komi
1980, 1984 parts (Adolf Turkin)

Latin
1986 (Tuomo Pekkanen)

Latvian
1924 (Linards Laicens)

Lithuanian
1922 (A. Sabaliauskas),
1972 (Justinas Marcinkevičius)

Low German
2001 (Herbert Strehmel)

Macedonian
1998 (Vesna Acevska)

Moldovian
1961, 1985 parts (P. Starostin)

Norwegian
1967 (Albert Lange Fliflet), etc.

Persian
1999 (Mersedeh Khadivar Mohseni &
Mahmoud Air Yar Ahmadi)

ר וּ נ וֹ ל "ג

יְצִיאָה לְפּוֹחְיוֹלָה לְהָבִיא מִשָּׁם אֶת הַסַּמְפּוֹ

אַחַר שֶׁרָאָה אִלְמָרִינֶן שֶׁלֹּא יוּכַל לְנַגֵּד לוֹ אִשָּׁה מִזָּהָב, קָם וְהָלַךְ
לְפּוֹחְיוֹלָה, אֶל לוֹחִי חֲמוֹתוֹ לְהִשְׁתַּדֵּךְ לְבִתָּהּ הַשְּׁנִיָּה. כַּאֲשֶׁר
שָׁמְעָה לוֹחִי, כִּי נִטְרְפָה בִּתָּהּ חֶמְדָּתָהּ וּמֵתָה, הֶאֱשִׁימָה אֶת
הַנַּפָּח שֶׁהוּא עַצְמוֹ הֲרָגָהּ. דַּי לָהּ שֶׁהִפְקִירָה אֶת בִּתָּהּ הָאַחַת
בְּתִתָּהּ אוֹתָהּ לוֹ לְאִשָּׁה, עַכְשָׁיו לֹא תִּתֵּן לוֹ אֶת הַשְּׁנִיָּה. בְּבֹשֶׁת
פָּנִים שִׁלְּחָה אוֹתוֹ מֵעַל פָּנֶיהָ. שָׁב הָאִישׁ עֲרִירִי וְאֻמְלָל אֶל
בֵּיתוֹ. בְּעוֹדוֹ בַּדֶּרֶךְ פָּגַשׁ בְּוֶנֶמֶּנֶן וְשָׁפַךְ לְפָנָיו אֶת מַר לִבּוֹ, נִסָּה
הָאִישׁ הֶחָכָם לְנַחֲמוֹ בְּצַעֲרוֹ, גַּם יָעֲצוֹ שֶׁיֵּלֶךְ לְפּוֹחְיוֹלָה וְיִקַּח

179

Polish
1965–1969, 1974 (Józef Ozga Michalski & Karol Laszecki)
1998 (Jerzy Litwiniuk), etc.

Portuguese
2007 (Orlando Moreira)
2010 (Ana Soares & Merja de Mattos-Pareira)

Romanian
1942 (Barbu B. Brezianu)
1959 (Julian Vesper), etc.

Russian
1888 (L. P. Belskij)
1998, 2006 (Eino Kiuru & Armas Mishin), etc.

Serbo-Croatian
1935, 1939 (Ivan Šajkovič), etc.

Slovakian
1962 parts (Marianna Prídavková-Mináriková & Miroslav Válek)
1986 (Marek Svetlik & Jan Petr Velkoborský)

Slovenian
1961 parts (Matej Rode & Severin Šali)
1997 Jelka Ovaska Novak & Bogdan Novak), etc.

Spanish
1953 (María Dolores Arroyo)
1984 Joaquin Fernández & Ursula Ojanen), etc.

Swahili
1992 parts (Jan Knappert)

14

Mache Kerben längs des Weges,
Wegezeichen an den Bäumen,   20
Daß ich Dummer richtig gehe,
Wildfremd hier die Wege finde,
Während ich die Beute suche,
5   Um die Gabe mich bemühe.

Waldes Wirtin, schöngestaltet,
Laß dein Wild nun vorwärts
                    wandern,
Laß das Silber sich bewegen
Vor dem Manne, der es suchet,
Auf dem Pfad des Spurenfolgers.
10

Kleingewachsne
                    Waldesjungfrau,   30
Honigmund'ge Tapiotochter!
Blase auf der Honigflöte,
Pfeife auf der süßen Pfeife
Vor der günst'gen Waldeswirtin,
15   Vor der gnäd'gen Wirtin
                    Ohren,   35
Denn sie hört mich ganz und
                    gar nicht
Und erwacht nicht aus dem Schlafe,

Ob ich auch beharrlich bitte
Und mit goldner Zunge rufe!"
Und der lust'ge
                    Lemminkäinen   40
Zieht beständig ohne Beute,
Eilt durch Sümpfe, eilt durch
                    Heiden,
25   Eilt durch überwilde Wälder.

Gleitet einen Tag, den zweiten;
Endlich an dem dritten Tage   45
Kommt er zu dem großen Berge,
Steigt er auf den steilen Felsen,
Wendet seinen Blick nach Westen,
Durch die Sümpfe hin nach
                    Südwest:
Sieht dort Tapios Tore
Goldne Fenster dorten glänzen.   50
Drauf der lust'ge
                    Lemminkäinen
35   Eilt sogleich nun hin zur Stelle,
Steht bald unter Tapios Fenstern,
Macht verborgen sich ans
                    Lauern.   55

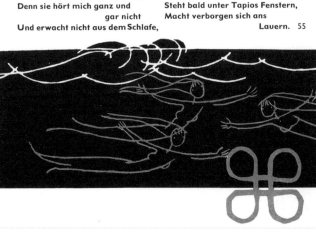

Kalevala in German. Translated by Anton Schiefner and Martin Buber. Illustrated by Bert Heller. Hinstorff Verlag, Rostock 1968.

Swedish
1841 (M. A. Castrén), 1884 (Rafaël Herzberg)
1999 (Lars Hulden & Mats Hulden), etc.

Tamil
1994, 1999 (Ramalingam Sivalingam)

Turkish
1965–1966, 1982 (Lâle & Muammer Obuz)

Udmurt
2001 parts (Anatoli Uvarov)

Ukranian
1901 (E. Timčenko)

Urdu
2012 (Arshad Farooq)

Vepsian
2003 parts (Nina Zaičeva)

Vietnamese
1986 parts (Cao Xuân Nghiêp)
1994 (Bùi Viêt Hoa), etc.

Yiddish
1954 parts (Hersh Rosenfeld)

Websites

Here is a selection of useful websites, which have a text option in English. You can also google the Kalevala and find something totally unexpected and surprising, such as readjusting the limbs in the kalevalaic fashion ('kalevalainen jäsenkorjaus').

The Kalevala pages of the Finnish Literature Society are in English (**www.finlit.fi/kalevala/english**).

   The Finnish Literature Society has digitised and published the original texts of folk poetry on the Internet. You can actually see what the published folk poetry materials used by Lönnrot were like. The book is called *Suomen Kansan Vanhat Runot* (The Ancient Poems of the Finnish People). It has 34 volumes, about 86,000 folklore texts, about 1.4 million lines in the kalevala-metre. The poems have been classified according to the area where the texts have been collected. The volumes were published between 1908 and 1948, plus an additional volume in 1997. **www.finlit.fi/skvr**

The Kalevala Society has a website in English. The website provides information on the society's activities in promoting Kalevala-inspired art and scholarly research. **www.kalevalaseura.fi**

Juminkeko is situated in Kuhmo, northeastern Finland. It is a foundation that promotes knowledge on the Kalevala, organises art exhibitions at its location, and visits to the villages of Archangel Karelia in Russia. They have a website in English. **www.juminkeko.fi**

The Gallen-Kallela Museum has a website in English. The museum is situated in Espoo, near Helsinki. It was once the studio of Akseli Gallen-Kallela, whose art includes kalevalaic themes. **www.gallen-kallela.fi**

The Ateneum Art Museum has an English website: **www.atenum.fi**

The collections of the museum include numerous works of art from the 'Golden Age' of Finnish art, as well as many Kalevala-related paintings and sculptures.

The Finnish National Museum has an English website: **www.nba.fi**

The collections extend from the Stone Age to the twentieth century. The ethnographic section 'A Land and its People' presents rural life in Finland before industrialisation (e.g. the entire interior of a smoke cabin) and a way of life similar to the one that Lönnrot encountered on his trips in the nineteenth century.

The Kalevala Women's Association is a cultural organisation with approximately 60 member organisations throughout Finland. It is intended for people with an interest in kalevala-metre poetry, Finnish traditional culture and its modern applications. The association publishes the journal Pirta. **www.kalevalaistennaistenliitto.fi**

The Kalevala has given impetus to progressive rock as well. A box set collection of three CDs has been released, first in 2004, a new edition in 2008: Kalevala – A Finnish Progressive Rock Epic. The website address: **www.prograrchives.com**

Established in 1990, Amorphis is an internationally known Finnish progressive metal band: **www.amorphis.net**
They have been influenced by Finnish mythology and themes from the Kalevala and the *Kanteletar*. They define their style as progressive metal, death metal, stoner rock and folk metal.

Värttinä – **www.varttina.com** – is internationally known as one of the most successful Finnish folk/pop music groups. Värttinä started out in Rääkkylä, North Karelia in 1983. Their music was originally based on Karelian and Finno-Ugric folk music, and they used kalevala-metre folk poetry in their lyrics.

The website Kulttuurisampo ('the Sampo of Culture') – **www.kulttuu-risampo.fi** – includes the semantic Kalevala, in which the events of the epic have been described for the computer with ontological concepts. The places and actors of the epic are included. The website functions in Finnish, but you can find some information in English too.

The Kalevala has been a source of inspiration for the architect Travis Price in his project 'Spirit of Place'. See **www.spiritofplace-design.com**

Select bibliography in English

Asplund, Anneli & Mettomäki, Sirkka-Liisa 1998: *Finfo: Kalevala 1835–1849–1999.* Kalevala Society and Finnish Literature Society. Helsinki: The Ministry of Foreign Affairs.

Beck, Brenda E. F. 1982. *The Three Twins. The Telling of a South Indian Folk Epic.* Bloomington: Indiana University Press.

Carpenter, Humphrey & Tolkien, Christian (eds.) 1981: *Letters of J. R. R. Tolkien. A Selection.* London: George Allen & Unwin.

Haavio, Martti 1952: *Väinämöinen: Eternal Sage.* Translated from Finnish by Helen Goldthwaith-Väänänen. Porvoo: WSOY.

Hearn, Lafcadio 1921: Note on the Influence of Finnish Poetry in English Literature. In: Erskine, John [ed.], *Books and Habits from the Lectures of Lafcadio Hearn.* New York: Dodd, Mead & Co.

Honko, Lauri 2002 (ed.): *Kalevala and the World´s Traditional Epics.* Studia Fennica Folkloristica 12. Helsinki: Suomalaisen Kirjallisuuden Seura.

Jaakkola, Jutta & Toivonen, Aarne (eds.) 2004: *Inspired by Tradition: Kalevala Poetry in Finnish Music.* Helsinki: The Finnish Music Information Centre.

Journal of Finnish Studies 2009. Volume 13, Number 2. [Toronto.]

Kalevala 1835–1985: The National Epic of Finland. Edited by Books from Finland, published by the Helsinki University Library.

Kirkinen, Heikki & Sihvo, Hannes 1985: *The Kalevala: An Epic of Finland and All Mankind.* Helsinki: Finnish-American Cultural Institute.

Kolehmainen, John I. 1973: *Epic of the North.* Minnesota: New York Mills.

Kuusi, Matti (ed.) 1995: *A Trail for Singers. Finnish Folk Poetry: Epic.* Translated by Keith Bosley. Helsinki: Finnish Literature Society.

Kuusi, Matti, Bosley, Keith, Branch, Michael (eds.) 1977: *Finnish Folk Poetry: Epic. An Anthology in Finnish and English.* Helsinki: Finnish Literature Society.

Lönnrot, Elias 1998: *The Kalevala. An Epic Poem After Oral Tradition by Elias Lönnrot.* Translated from the Finnish with an Introduction and Notes by Keith Bosley, and a Foreword by Albert B. Lord. Oxford World's Classics. Oxford: Oxford University Press.

Mäkinen, Kirsti 2009: *The Kalevala – Tales of Magic and Adventure.* The Kalevala retold by Kirsti Mäkinen, translated by Kaarina Brooks and illustrated by Pirkko-Liisa Surojegin. Vancouver: Simply Read Books.

Oinas, Felix J. 1985: *Studies in Finnic Folklore. Homage to the Kalevala.* Helsinki: Suomalaisen Kirjallisuuden Seura.

Ojanperä, Riitta (ed.) 2009: *The Kalevala in Images.* Helsinki: Ateneum Art Museum.

Pentikäinen, Juha Y. 1999: *Kalevala Mythology.* Expanded Edition, translated and edited by Ritva Poom. Bloomington and Indianapolis: Indiana University Press.

Siikala, Anna-Leena 2002: *Mythic Images and Shamanism. A Perspective on Kalevala Poetry.* FF Communications 280. Helsinki: Suomalainen Tiedeakatemia/ Academia Scientiarum Fennica.

Siikala, Anna-Leena & Vakimo, Sinikka (eds.) 1994: *Songs Beyond the Kalevala.* Studia Fennica Folkloristica. Helsinki: Suomalaisen Kirjallisuuden Seura.

Wilson, William 1976: *Folklore and Nationalism in Modern Finland.* Bloomington: Indiana University Press.

Select bibliography in Finnish

Annist, August 1944: *Kalevala taideteoksena*. Translated by Elsa Haavio. Helsinki: WSOY.

Anttila, Aarne 1985: *Elias Lönnrot. Elämä ja toiminta.* Suomalaisen Kirjallisuuden Seuran toimituksia 417. 2. painos. Helsinki: Suomalaisen Kirjallisuuden Seura.

Anttonen, Pertti & Kuusi, Matti 1999: *Kalevala–lipas.* Uusi laitos. Suomalaisen Kirjallisuuden Seuran toimituksia 740. Helsinki: Suomalaisen Kirjallisuuden Seura.

Ganander, Christfried 1984: *Mythologia Fennica.* Facsimile. 4th edition. Helsinki: Suomalaisen Kirjallisuuden Seura.

Honko, Lauri (ed.) 1987: *Kalevala ja maailman eepokset.* Kalevalaseuran vuosikirja 65. NIF Publications 16. Helsinki: Suomalaisen Kirjallisuuden Seura.

Jalkanen, Pekka & Laitinen, Heikki & Tenhunen, Anna-Liisa 2010: *Kantele.* Editor: Risto Blomster. Helsinki: Suomalaisen Kirjallisuuden Seura.

Jussila, Raimo 2009: *Kalevalan sanakirja.* Helsinki: Otava.

Kaukonen, Väinö 1979: *Lönnrot ja Kalevala.* Suomalaisen Kirjallisuuden Seuran toimituksia 349. Helsinki: Suomalaisen Kirjallisuuden Seura.

Kuusi, Matti & Anttonen, Pertti 1985: *Kalevala-lipas.* Suomalaisen Kirjallisuuden Seuran toimituksia 413. Helsinki: Suomalaisen Kirjallisuuden Seura.

Laaksonen, Pekka (ed.) 1984: *Lönnrotin aika.* Kalevalaseuran vuosikirja 64. Helsinki: Suomalaisen Kirjallisuuden Seura.

Laaksonen, Pekka & Mettomäki, Sirkka-Liisa (eds.) 2002: *Pyhän perintö. Kirjoituksia suomalaisesta pyhästä Kalevalassa, kansanperinteessä, luonnossa ja taiteessa.* Kalevalaseuran vuosikirja 79–80. Helsinki: Suomalaisen Kirjallisuuden Seura.

Laaksonen, Pekka & Piela, Ulla (eds.) 2002: *Lönnrotin hengessä.* Kalevalaseuran vuosikirja 81. Helsinki: Suomalaisen Kirjallisuuden Seura.

Lönnrot, Elias 1952: *Vaeltaja. Muistelmia jalkamatkalta Hämeestä, Savosta ja Karjalasta 1828.* Helsinki: Suomalaisen Kirjallisuuden Seura.

Lönnrot, Elias 1964: *Kalevala.* Uuden Kalevalan 24. painos. Suomalaisen Kirjallisuuden Seuran toimituksia 14. Helsinki: Suomalaisen Kirjallisuuden Seura.

Lönnrot, Elias 1982: *Kanteletar elikkä Suomen kansan vanhoja lauluja ja virsiä.* 14. painos. Helsinki: Suomalaisen Kirjallisuuden Seura.

Lönnrot, Elias 1999: *Kalevala 1835. Kalevala taikka vanhoja Karjalan runoja Suomen kansan muinosista ajoista.* 1835 julkaistun *Kalevalan* laitoksen uusi painos. Helsinki: Suomalaisen Kirjallisuuden Seura.

Nieminen, Kai 1999: *Kalevala 1999.* Elias Lönnrotin 1849 ilmestyneen Kalevalan pohjalta kirjoittanut Kai Nieminen, kuvittanut Adam Korpak. Helsinki: Suomalaisen Kirjallisuuden Seura.

Ojanperä, Riitta (ed.) 2009: *Kalevala kuvissa. 160 vuotta Kalevalan innoittamaa suomalaista taidetta.* Helsinki: Ateneumin taidemuseo / Valtion taidemuseo.

Piela, Ulla & Knuuttila, Seppo & Kupiainen, Tarja (eds.) 1999: *Kalevalan hyvät ja hävyttömät.* Suomalaisen Kirjallisuuden Seuran toimituksia 746. Suomalaisen Kirjallisuuden Seura: Helsinki.

Piela, Ulla & Knuuttila, Seppo & Laaksonen, Pekka (eds.) 2008: *Kalevalan kulttuurihistoria.* Helsinki: Suomalaisen Kirjallisuuden Seura.

Porthan, Henrik Gabriel 1983: *Suomalaisesta runoudesta.* Suom. Iiro Kajanto. Helsinki: Suomalaisen Kirjallisuuden Seura.

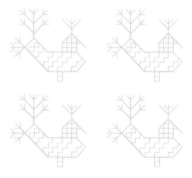

Salminen, Väinö 1947: *Kalevala-kirja.* Toinen, uudistettu painos. Helsinki: Otava.

Sarmela, Matti 1994: *Suomen perinneatlas.* Suomen kansankulttuurin kartasto 2. Suomalaisen Kirjallisuuden Seuran toimituksia 587. Helsinki: Suomalaisen Kirjallisuuden Seura.

Siikala, Anna-Leena 1992: *Suomalainen šamanismi — mielikuvien historiaa.* Helsinki: Suomalasen Kirjallisuuden Seura.

Siikala, Anna-Leena & Harvilahti, Lauri & Timonen, Senni (eds.) 2004: *Kalevala ja laulettu runo.* Suomalaisen Kirjallisuuden Seuran toimituksia 958. Helsinki: Suomalaisen Kirjallisuuden Seura.

Turunen, Aimo 1981: *Kalevalan sanat ja niiden taustat.* Joensuu: Karjalaisen kulttuurin edistämissäätiö.